TALKS

by
Swami Paramatmananda Puri

VOLUME 1

Revised Edition – 2015

Mata Amritanandamayi Center
San Ramon, California, United States

Talks
Volume 1 - Revised Edition
by Swami Paramatmananda Puri

Published by:
Mata Amritanandamayi Center
P.O. Box 613
San Ramon, CA 94583-0613, USA

In India:
www.amritapuri.org
inform@amritapuri.org

In USA:
www.amma.org

In Europe:
www.amma-europe.org

Preface

To
JAGADGURU
Sri Mata Amritanandamayi Devi
with deep devotion, respectful regards,
and reverential salutations

Since 1968, Swami Paramatmananda Puri has lived the life of a renunciate in India, moving there at the age of nineteen, to imbibe the spiritual essence of that great and ancient culture. It has been his good fortune to have kept the company of many saints and sages over the years, culminating in his meeting with his Guru, Mata Amritanandamayi, in 1979. As one of her senior disciples, he was eventually asked to return to the U.S. to serve as head of the first ashram in the West, the Mata Amritanandamayi Center, where he remained in residence since from 1990 until 2001.

Many residents and visitors to the Center have shared that one of the high points in programs there have been Swami is talks, encompassing Amma is teachings, his experiences in India, his understanding of scriptural texts, and his life on the spiritual path. With wit and humour, he has synthesized East and West, and created a forum for spiritual learning for people from all walks of life.

Originally available only on tape, his talks have now been transcribed, with his speaking style preserved as much as possible, making these volumes a treasury of wisdom for years to come.

These talks were recorded over twenty years ago. For this revised edition, Swamiji decided to rewrite the book in a more readable style.

Publisher
Amritapuri, India
August 1, 2017

Contents

Stories of Saints - 1

SPIRITUAL GIANTS OF INDIA ARE NOT LIMITED TO monastics alone. There have been many married *mahatmas*, particularly those who lived long ago during Vedic times, who were known as *rishis* or sages. We shouldn't think that every mahatma has to be a *sannyasi*, that one cannot become a saint, a sage or a mystic unless one renounces the world and puts on *gerua* or orange cloth. There have been many realized people who were married and worked in order to support their family. In all their free time, they would do *sadhana* or spiritual practice. They looked upon their daily life as an opportunity to develop spiritually.

You Can't Take It With You

I knew a philosophy professor who lived in Hyderabad in Andhra. He was fortunate to have a job that was conducive to his spiritual life. Whenever he didn't have to talk or engage himself in something—if he was just sitting alone or was in a bus on the way somewhere or was driving his car—one could see that one of his hands was tapping his leg as if counting. In fact, he was doing *japa* (repetition) of the Divine Name "Ram." Every free moment, he was doing japa. He used to visit every saint or sage that came to Hyderabad in order to have their *darshan*. He would invite them to visit or stay at his house. Some sannyasis and saints stayed there for two or three years. The rest of his family wasn't very happy about it, but he didn't really care about their opinion. He had realized that, while in this perishable world, he must make the most of his possessions by using them in such a way that they would benefit him spiritually. He converted all his worldly assets to *punyam* (religious merit).

According to Indian tradition, all the desire-prompted actions done with our body, speech and mind create reactions or karmsa that are either positive (*punya*), negative (*papa*), or neutral. Punya results in future happiness and papa brings about future suffering. The comforts and pleasures of this life are the results of past lives' punya, while pain and sorrow are the result of papa. The unseen results of our actions follow us from birth to birth; there is a kind of 'account' into which the results of our karmas go birth after birth. This is called *sanchita* (accumulated actions from all our past births). Although the common understanding is that 'you can't take it with you,' in fact, we can and we do! By leading a virtuous or *dharmic* life, we build up our stock or account of punya. In fact, we can even convert the assets of this life, such as wealth and possessions, into punyam. But this must be done before we leave our body. As far as I have understood, assets that are bequeathed after death do not count in this calculation. Part of the reason an action becomes punya is because of the self-sacrifice and detachment required to do it, however little.

Suppose we want to go to a country that does not have a foreign exchange system. The conversion must be done here first for our money to become valid currency there. Our actions, our wealth, our health, and everything, can be converted to punyam, but only here and now. We can't do it later. Afterwards, when we're on the other side, when we've left our body and reached the other world, no one is going to ask us, "Would you like us to convert your earthly assets to our currency here?" So whatever we want to be converted, we have to convert it here and now.

Of course, there is ordinary punya and then there is spiritual punya. Actions performed out of the desire for purification of the mind through divine grace leading to God-realization yield just that. They do not bear fruit in the form of worldly pleasure. So, some great spiritual beings who were householders did just that; they realized that life is fleeting, that any moment it may end, and so they got the most out of life. But this was not in the sense that most people think of getting the most out of life. They prepared for the lives after this life.

Karaikkal Ammaiyar and the Mangoes

During the sixth century in Tamil Nadu, a great lady saint named Punithavathiar, took birth. She later became famous as Karaikkal Ammaiyar, the 'Respected Mother from Karaikkal'. In Tamil Nadu, there exists an ancient tradition or line of sixty-three saints, called the Nayanmars who were all great devotees of Lord Shiva during the sixth to eighth centuries. In Shiva temples, one can see not only the image of the Lord but also of these great devotees lined up on one side of the inner part of the temple. They wrote many devotional songs and were all mystics who received the Lord's grace in the form of direct experience of His existence. Punithavathiar was one of the first among them. Her life illustrates the truth of Amma's words that innocence draws Divine Grace to oneself.

Punithavathiar was the daughter of a wealthy merchant. Her childless parents were very pious devotees of Lord Shiva and had prayed to Him for a child. She grew up into a very beautiful girl endowed with devotion just like her parents. In due course, she was married to another merchant's son by the name of Parama-dattan. They had been living a happy and contented life when something happened that changed everything for both of them.

One day, when the husband was sitting in his shop, some friends came and gave him two big juicy mangoes, which he gave to his servant, telling him to take them home and give them to his wife. She was to be told that Paramadattan would have them with lunch when he came.

She had just finished cooking the rice but nothing else, when a *sadhu*, a Shiva devotee, called out in front of her house,

> *"Annapurne sadapurne sankara prana vallabhe*
> *jñanavairagya siddhyartham bhiksham dehi ca parvati"*

Meaning:

> "Annapurna Devi, Goddess of Plenty, you are Lord Shiva's eternal Consort, give us alms together with wisdom."

He was begging for food and, since she was a devotee of Shiva, she naturally she wanted to feed him. She came running to the door and said, "Swami, please, come in and sit down." What was she going to serve with the rice? There were probably some pickles in the kitchen but nothing else. Then she remembered the mangoes. She thought, 'I'll give him one mango as a side dish, and maybe some yogurt and he can mix the whole thing; it'll be delicious.' So she took one of the mangoes and gave it to the sadhu. He ate all the rice and the mango; he was very happy, blessed her, and went his away.

After some time, the husband came home, had his bath and sat down for lunch. Punithavathiar served him rice along with all the items that she had prepared.

"What about that mangos? I sent some mangoes, didn't I?"

"Yes, I'll bring one." She went and brought the remaining mango and put it on his plate.

"Wow, this is delicious. Bring the other one also."

Now she was in a fix. She didn't say anything. She could have said something at that time. She could've said, "I gave it to a sadhu," but somehow she was a little hesitant. She wanted to please her husband. So she went into the storeroom and started crying, "O Shiva, O Shiva—what am I to do? He's asking for the mango and I don't have the mango. I could've told him why but I didn't. Now what am I to say?" She raised her hands and cried, "O God, please save me!" And then, suddenly, a mango manifested in her hands. Naturally, she was a little wonderstruck, but more than that, very grateful that the Lord had saved the day. She took the mango and gave it to her husband.

He ate it and said, "Hey, this is ten times as sweet as the first one. Where did you get this? Is this the same mango that I sent? How could I have given two mangoes that are so completely different? This is amazing."

Now she thought she'd better tell the truth, so she said, "A sadhu came begging and there was nothing but rice to give him, so I gave the first mango. When you asked for the second mango now, I prayed to Lord Shiva and He gave me the second one."

"Right. So since He gave you the second mango, can you get another one from Him also?" he asked sarcastically.

"I don't know. I'll pray." She went back inside the kitchen and started crying, "O Lord! Please save me from this situation!" And then another mango appeared in her hands! She came out and offered it to her husband.

He took it in his hand, but it disappeared as soon as he touched it. Now he was not only shocked but afraid also, because he realized that his wife was not an ordinary lady. "Are you a goddess?" he asked.

But she didn't say anything. She didn't know what to say.

So, then and there, he made a decision that since his wife seemed to be a goddess and not an ordinary lady, he could not live with her as his wife. Being a merchant, he used to travel across the seas in his ships, so he left on the next ship and never returned to Karaikkal. Eventually, he settled down in Madurai, which was quite a distance away from his native place. He married again and had a daughter, whom he named after as his first wife, Punithavathiar.

In the meantime, Punithavathiar was waiting for her husband to come home. After five or six years, some of her relatives who had been to Madurai and seen him there told her, "We saw your husband and he is in Madurai." They decided to send her there, and hired a palanquin. So off she went along with some of them. They also sent word to him that she was coming.

When Punithavathiar arrived, Paramadattan came running out with his second wife and his daughter to meet her. As soon as she got out of the palanquin, what did he do? He made a *sashtanga namaskaram*, prostrating fully stretched out at her feet in great respect. She didn't like that very much, to say the least. Before this, as an Indian wife, it was she who was bowing down to his feet.

She exclaimed, "What is this? What are you doing?!"

Then he told the whole story to her relatives:

"This lady is not an ordinary woman but a goddess, and, by her grace, I got remarried and got a child, and so I worship her in my house as the goddess Punithavathiar."

Hearing this, she felt so upset that she prayed intensely to Lord Shiva: "O Lord, I was preserving my beauty for my husband and now he doesn't want me anymore. So let only You be my all in all. Take away my beauty."

Immediately, she became all shriveled up and skinny, almost like a ghost. They say she became ghoul-like and very strange looking. Seeing her new appearance, everybody ran away in fear. But she was very happy, because this was the beginning of her life of total renunciation. It was God's will, not hers.

She then began a long pilgrimage and walked all the way to Mount Kailas in the Himalayas. In those days, making a distant pilgrimage was a dangerous affair. One may have to go through forests infested with wild animals, or worse, wild humans!

Reaching Kailas, the Lord blessed her with His mystic vision or darshan. He asked her, "What would you like? I'll give you a boon."

"I want constant *bhakti*. I want total, permanent, continuous devotion to You. I think of so many things, my mind wanders around from one thing to another. I want that it should flow only towards You without a break, just as the Ganga river flows towards the ocean.

"I don't want to be reborn anymore; there's nothing in this world that I want. I only want to be at Your Feet. And if I have to be reborn due to some *karma*, then let me always be conscious that You exist; let me not fall asleep anymore in Your Maya so that I forget that You exist and think that only this world is real and of value. Let me be God-conscious even though I am reborn."

And, finally, she prayed that she should be able to see the Cosmic Dance of the Lord at all times. This could mean two different things. You might have seen the image of Lord Shiva as Nataraja, the King of dance. He is dancing with fire blazing all around Him. This represents the dance of the universe. Every single thing in the universe is moving. There is nothing that is absolutely still; every atom is in motion. Shakti or Mother Nature is constantly dancing. Nature dances into existence, and dances out of existence also. When vibrations stop, that's the end of Creation. Then comes *pralaya*, the dissolution of the universe. And after that, the dance starts again.

This is one way of interpreting what she wanted to see as the Cosmic Dance of God. In other words, she wanted to see the whole universe as the form of God. The other interpretation may be that she wanted to actually see the form of Nataraja, as Lord Shiva dancing in the *akasha*, in space. And so Shiva said, "Yes, you'll have that vision and everything you asked for." He then told her to go back to Tamil Nadu to a holy place called

Tiruvalangadu where there is a Shiva temple said to be one of the places that the Lord dances His Cosmic Dance, and to stay there. She spent the rest of her life there in meditation and ecstasy and attained Liberation by the grace of Lord Shiva.

Karaikkal Ammaiyar wrote more than a hundred songs that describe her spiritual experiences and mystic union with God. This is part of the Saiva literature, the literature of the Nayanmars.

The Woman Who Fed Baby Rama

I used to spend a lot of time in Hyderabad for the first ten or twelve years I was in India. At that time, I met a woman devotee of Ramana Maharshi who seemed like an ordinary lady. She was a brahmin widow and used to spend all her time either doing puja, studying the *Srimad Bhagavata* and other scriptures, or doing japa. She used to repeat the name of God a hundred thousand times a day. She would get up about three o'clock in the morning and from then, until nine or ten o'clock, she would sit there like a statue doing japa. As you can imagine, she made great progress and started to experience divine visions.

During the mid-seventy's she came and settled down in Tiru-vannamalai. Somehow, we became friends. Though she was very orthodox, she showed a lot of affection towards me, like an elder sister towards her younger brother. Some days, she would come and cook for me, and afterwards, we would talk about spiritual matters. I could speak her language, Telugu, a bit at that time. I used to speak in a very simple way and she'd speak in a very simple way, and she used to tell me about her experiences.

Sometimes you talk to people—so-called spiritual people—and they start to talk about all their experiences, you feel as if either there's something wrong with them, or they're trying to impress you. A lot of people talk like that. But if you talk to a genuine, innocent person, you don't feel like that at all. You can tell that they're like a child. Real spiritual people are like children. This lady was just like a child, and after we knew each other for some time, she started telling me what was happening to her during her present sadhana.

She said that she felt very upset because, as a devotee of Ramana Maharshi, she liked to do *atma vichara*, self-enquiry. But every time she would close her eyes and try to hold onto the I-thought, to try to see the Atman, a little boy would show up—baby Rama, a tiny, three-year-old light-grey-blue Rama. He would come and jump onto her lap and would start to tug at her clothes, and say, "I want some *payasam* (sweet pudding)! I want *vadai* (fried gram cake). I want *dosa* (a fried pancake). I want something to eat!" She could actually she see this; she would feel her clothes being tugged at, and hear him crying. But as soon as she would open her eyes, he would disappear. And when she would close her eyes, again she would see him and feel his pulling at her and hear him crying, and she was very upset.

While hearing this amazing story, all I could think was how happy I would be if something like that happened to me. At least something would be happening when I closed my eyes, something other than thoughts and sleep! But that was the difference between us—she wasn't going to settle for anything less than Self-realization, *Atma Jñana*. She didn't even want the vision of Rama or Krishna or anybody else.

Usually, she wouldn't have to cook at that hour. It was too early in the morning. But if she didn't cook and get the food ready, Rama wouldn't leave her alone. So she'd cook the payasam and the vadai. She didn't want it for herself; after all, she was just a simple spiritual aspirant. But for *him* she had to cook all these fancy dishes; he simply wouldn't settle for anything less. And then, with her eyes closed, she had to feed him, because she could only see him when her eyes were closed. She couldn't even get any rest, because if she closed her eyes to sleep, he would come and lay down next to her, cuddling up against her, wanting to play and hear stories!

She was very upset and used to tell me about it. She said, "What's going to be my fate? I wanted to realize the Self, and I have to be playing with God all the time? He keeps me cooking—every morning at four o'clock in the morning I have to cook like this. What am I to do?"

And what was I to say to her? That was even more difficult, because I had no idea—I wasn't seeing Rama, Krishna or Shiva! So I said, "Surrender to God's will." What else could I say?

Finally, one day, she came and said, "You know, last night a beautiful thing happened. I was meditating, and Rama again came, and I was a little—I don't know, I was getting frustrated; I didn't know what to do anymore. So I started praying to my Guru, and my Guru appeared there, and he had a big cooking pot."

(A huge pot, it was big enough to stand up in. I have seen some of the cooking pots in India, where they cook for feasts; to clean the pot one has to get inside and stand in it, it's so big. There was a big pot like that.)

"Then he had a big stick and he was stirring whatever it was—I don't know what it was. And I was looking at it and wondering, 'What a strange thing Guruji is doing; I wonder what he's cooking?' Then he called me over, and I looked in the pot, and he said, 'This is Mysore Pak'—Mysore Pak is a kind of sweet— 'It's Mysore pak, but it's not ready.'"

Then she understood what he was talking about: that she wasn't ripe yet for Self-enquiry. The sweet—that's the sweet mind, the evolved mind, the spiritual mind. So he's stirring it but it's not ready, it's not completely cooked. If it hadn't been cooking at all, she wouldn't have seen Rama. But because it was boiling and cooking, she was getting that vision. Then she said that after this vision, the vision of Rama as a baby boy stopped, and her mind became still, like a calm ocean, and she was able to sit for hours and hours immersed in herself, in the Atman.

This was just an apparently ordinary lady; nobody knew about her experiences—I might be the only person that knew. I never told anybody. In fact, you're the first people I ever told that to. I'm so sure that she wasn't telling anybody, because she had no friends. She didn't care about friends; she cared only about spiritual practice.

There must be so many devotees like this lady, so many saints. One of Ramakrishna Paramahamsa's woman disciples had the same "problem". Some problem!

The Lady Who Cured the Swiss Boy's Ear

One day, some of us were sitting with Amma in front of the ashram. Sitting some distance away, there was also a Swiss boy, who had been living in the ashram for some years. He would spend a lot of time meditating. As a result, his body overheated and he developed an ear infection.

As we were talking, a beggar-lady arrived on the scene. Sometimes beggars would cross the backwaters to beg food in the village. It looked as if she had not had a bath or changed her dirty and torn clothes in years. She seemed to be in her seventies, bent over holding a little tin can in her hand for begging. She went right over to the Swiss boy and leaned over as if she was going to say something. And then, whoosh, whoosh, she blew into his infected! Without waiting for anyone to give her anything, she just smiled at him and left the place, as if she had come just for that purpose.

Amma had been watching the whole scene and then turned to us and said, "Did you see that?"

We saw it but didn't know what it was we were looking at.

"You know who that is?"

"Nope."

"She's never come here before," said Amma.

"Then, Amma, how did you know who she is?"

Without thinking, we always seem to ask this stupid question to Amma. The next moment, we usually realize what a fool we are to ask her how she knows something. She knows because her knowledge is born of intuition, not born of experience, inference or intellect Anyhow, we asked her,

"Amma, how do you know?"

"That was an *avadhuta*, a lady mahatma. She wanders around like a beggar. It's the first time she's ever come here, yet she knew that his ear was infected, and that was the only reason she came. She didn't come here to beg food from us. Didn't you see the way she just blew in his ear and went away?" She paused and added, "There are many people like that. In fact, there's probably one in each village, but we just don't know about them because they look like ordinary people."

Mayamma

Appearances can be deceiving. We are all familiar with the saying that all that glitters is not gold. It is also true that those who do not glitter may actual be gold! Many of you might have heard of Mayamma, a lady avadhuta who was living in Tamil Nadu until recently (she passed away 9th of February, 1992). Amma spent some time with her. We used to go and visit her once in two or three years. She was also like that. She looked like a beggar. She used to walk around with a gunny bag, and with the gunny bag she would run into hotels, pull people's food off their plates, put it into the bag, and then run out of the hotel. We had no place to eat when we went to see her, so we went to a restaurant. One of the devotees had just ordered her breakfast and gotten up to go to the bathroom. Just then, Mayamma ran into the hotel, took everything off of her plate, and ran out.

What did she do with the food? She didn't eat it herself. There were about twenty-five dogs that followed her around. She slept on the dogs, lay down on the dogs, played with the dogs, and fed the dogs. This was how she fed the dogs—by getting the food from the hotels. No hotel owner would stop her, because they considered it a blessing that a saint with such spiritual power chose to come into their shop. Nobody knew how old she was, but Amma said that she was more than a hundred and fifty years old. If she touched somebody who was sick, they would become all right.

She swam in the ocean without any clothes on. Some people put clothes on her, but she didn't seem to like that. She would wander through the town and nobody would disturb her. She collected heaps of garbage from the city, dumped it on the ocean side, lit it, and sat there gazing at it for some hours. Nobody knew what she was doing. Amma said that she was a great mahatma, and so we believed that she must be. There is a saying that only a Realized Soul can understand another Realized Soul.

There have been many great saintly women like Mayamma. I wanted to talk about one of the greatest, but we have run out of time. We'll have to wait till next time. We will be talking about Andal. She was one of the greatest. There have been great ones, and then there have been greater ones still. All of them have experienced God, but Andal was unique.

Stories of Saints - 2

Saint Tulasidas

MANY OF US MIGHT HAVE HEARD OF TULASIDAS. He wrote a great book, *Tulasi Ramayana*, or *Ramacharitamanasa*, which is a devotional version of the original Ramayana written by Valmiki.

Tulasidas was a great devotee of Lord Rama and spent many years trying to get His vision but, in spite of all his efforts, couldn't get it. Every day, he used to go to the Ganges River to get some water so that after he would go to the toilet he would have the water to clean himself. As he was walking back, he used to throw the remainder of the water at the foot of one tree. One day, as he was passing the tree after throwing the water, he heard a voice say, "I'll give you a boon." He couldn't understand where was this voice coming from. So he went near the tree again and the voice said, "I'll give you a boon. What boon do you want?"

Then Tulasidas asked, "Who is this that's talking?"

"I am a ghost who is possessing this tree—who lives in this tree—and I've been very thirsty, and am grateful to you because you've been giving me this water every day. So, whatever I can do for you, name it. I'll give you a boon."

"I would like the darshan of Rama."

"I can't do that for you, but I know somebody who can. That is Hanuman."

"I also know that, by Hanuman's grace, I can see Rama, but where is he?"

"Every evening you're giving a discourse on the Ramayana, and the last person to leave after the discourse is over is a leper who is in the back of the room; that's Hanuman. He's coming just to enjoy the story of Rama, and he comes disguised like that. So go there and appeal to him for Rama's darshan."

So Tulasidas waited that night until after everybody had gotten up and left. He saw the last person to get up was a leper at the back of the room, so he went over to him, fell at his feet, and, holding his feet, cried, "O Hanumanji, please bless me with your grace!"

The leper just stood there and finally said, "I am nobody. Why are you bowing to me?"

"No, I know you are Hanumanji." He kept persisting, and then, finally, Hanumanji said, "Okay, what do you want?"

"I want Ram's darshan."

"All right, go to Chitrakoot." That was the mountain where Rama and Sita used to live for many years, and which was not too far from where Tulasidas was at the time. "Go to Chitrakoot and worship Rama there, and you'll get Rama's darshan by my grace."

Tulasidas followed Hanuman's advice, and, sure enough, got the darshan of Rama twice, but in a very strange way. During the first darshan, Tulasidas was sitting and doing Ram puja when a boar came running there, knocked over everything, and went off. To say the least, he was very upset—his puja was spoiled, and everything was dirty and stinking.

Hanuman soon arrived and said, "Well, did you see Ram?"

"I didn't see Ram. Where is Ram? I've been sitting here doing puja and I still haven't seen Rama. You promised me!"

"That boar was Him. He just ran through your puja."

"If He looks like that, how am I to recognize Him?"

"Okay, you'll get the darshan of Rama one more time."

So Tulasidas did the puja another day. At the conclusion, many people came there to get the *prasad*. Two young boys came there; one was fair and one was dark. Tulasidas was giving the prasad to everybody, and as he put the *chandanam* (sandalwood paste) on the forehead of these two boys, just as he touched them, he realized that they were Rama and Lakshmana. He became unconscious with ecstasy and lay there for two or three days in the bliss of having seen his Lord.

Anybody may be anything—a god or a demon. We cannot tell who is who. Mahatmas don't wear signs saying: "I am a great soul." In truth, everybody is a manifestation of the Divine. Through spiritual practice, we can actually experience that. Until then, it is a good idea to develop that attitude at all times.

Unniappam Swami

There was a very strange character living in the coastal area named Unniappam Swami. Most people thought he was a beggar, but he had one unusual quality that made him stand out as anything but a beggar. He had matted hair tied on his head, which is not unusual in itself—many sadhus do—but when he was walking along the seacoast, little kids would come and play and make fun of him—you know how little kids are. He would not get irritated, but, on the other hand, he would just stick his hands in his hair and pull out ready-cooked hot *unniappams* and give them to all the kids. Unniappam is a kind of a sweet they cook in Kerala. He used to 'cook' them in his own way. This is how he got the name "Unniappam Swami."

One day, he was walking down the seacoast and entered the village where Amma was born. This happened just before she was born. At that time, Amma's mother, Damayanti Amma, was pregnant with her. They were living just near the path that goes through the village along the ocean side, not where the ashram is now. Damayanti Amma was standing in front of the house when Unniappam Swami walked by. He came over to her and gave her some sacred ashes (*vibhuti, bhasma*). He said, "Parashakti (the Supreme Power) is in your womb and She will be born as your daughter." And then he just walked away. Now, of course, there are millions of people that have experienced Amma as the Divine Mother, but if you had seen Unniappam Swami in those days, you wouldn't have imagined he could know such a thing.

Under the Present Ashram

When Amma's father, Sugunanandan, had been a young man, he was playing with a friend of his in the front yard on a cashew tree when and a sadhu came there and started laughing and laughing.

The young boy asked him, "Why are you laughing? Are you making fun of us?"

"No, I'm laughing because I feel so blissful here. This is a holy place, and, under this earth, so there are many tombs of holy people—so many monks have been buried under here. There must have been an ashram here long ago." And then he just left the place.

Amma says that it is so—that under the present ashram, her ashram from her previous existence was there. This is one of the reasons we feel so much peace and bliss there. Of course, the fact that Amma has been living there her whole life, and that so many *sadhaks* are doing sadhana there greatly contributes to the peace and power of the place.

Mahatmas Can Be Any Age

We need not think that only old people can be mahatmas; young people also can be so. Take Amma, for example. Since she was a teenager, she had been manifesting the *bhava darshans*, and even though not everybody understood it, most people did accept that she was a great soul. Sri Suka Brahman, Sri Ramakrishna Paramahamsa and Sri Ramana Maharshi were all mahatmas even in their youth.

You might have read the story of Nachiketas in the *Kathopanishad*. It is a classical story of how a young person could be a great saint. For those of you who don't know the story of Nachiketas, I'd like to talk about it and also read a little bit from the Kathopanishad.

Nachiketas and the Lord of Death

Nachiketas had been a teenager at the time when his father decided to perform a big ritual worship or *puja*. In India, when a big puja is performed, part of the puja includes giving gifts to the priests. Nachiketas' father didn't have much money, but he had some completely dried up cows. They had no milk and no calves. What's anybody going to do with a dried up old cow? Yet he gave all these old cows away to the priests as if it was a very great gift. Seeing this travesty of dharma, Nachiketas, who had studied the scriptures and had strong faith in the Vedas, couldn't keep quiet. He felt that he must say something to his father because what was he was doing was against dharma. He knew that, if you give something that's useless to someone, you'll get a bad result in the future, and if you give a good thing, you'll get a good result.

So, to protect his father, he said, "Father, this isn't so good. Maybe you could give me away to them instead." The father didn't say anything. Then again he said, "Father, who are you going to give me to?"

The father didn't say anything. Nachiketas said it three or four times. Finally, his father got angry with him. "I give you to Yama, to Death." Nachiketas said, "Okay." He left and went to the abode of Death, the Yamaloka. But on reaching there, Yama was not there in his palace. So Nachiketas sat there at the gate for three days and three nights.

When Yama finally came, he was shocked to see Nachiketas. "Oh, this poor boy, he's been sitting here three days!" He immediately invited him inside the palace and said, "Listen, I want to do something for you, because you're my guest and you've been suffering three days and three nights sitting at my gate with no food, no water, nothing. So I'll give you three boons."

What were the boons?

Nachiketas said, "Okay, my first boon: I would like when I go back home, that my father shouldn't be angry at me anymore."

Yama said, "Okay, so be it. What do you want for the second boon?"

"I heard that in Heaven there's no suffering, there's no sorrow, there's not even death like there is on earth. So I'd like to know how to get to Heaven—what's the means to get to Heaven."

Yama told him, "There is a kind of worship that you have to do. If you do that puja, then you will go to Heaven after you leave the body." Then he taught him how to do the worship—it was actually a fire ceremony—and said, "And in honor of you, I'm going to name this as the Nachiketas fire ceremony. What would you like for your third boon?"

Yama asked, "What do you like for your third boon?"

Nachiketas said, "When a person dies, there arises this doubt whether he still exists. Some say he doesn't exist. I want you to teach me the truth. This is my third boon."

Some people say when you die, that's the end of everything—that's what materialists say. And some people say you still exist after death. So, since you're the god of death, you must know better than anybody else. I want to know what happens after death. Well, am I going to exist or not?

Yama said, "This doubt haunted even the gods, for the secret of death is hard to know. Nachiketas, ask for some other boon, and release me from my promise. Don't ask me this, please."

Nachiketas said, "This doubt haunted even the gods of old—because it is hard to know, O Death, as you say; I can have no greater teacher than you, and there is no boon equal to this. So, I don't want anything else, I want to know what happens after death."

Yama said, "Ask for sons and grandsons who will live a hundred years; ask for herds of cattle, elephants, horses, gold, land. Ask to live as long as you desire, or if you can think of anything more desirable, ask for that, with wealth and long life as well, Nachiketas. Be the ruler of a great kingdom, and I'll give you the utmost capacity to enjoy the pleasures of life."

What's he doing? Bribing him? Well, let's not use that word. Tempting him. But, yes, you could say, sort of, he's bribing him. But Naachiketas was too clever.

Nachiketas said, "These pleasures last only till tomorrow, and they wear out the vital power of life. How fleeting is all life on earth. Therefore, keep your horses and your chariots, your dancing and your music for yourself. Never can mortals be happy by wealth alone. How can we be desirous of wealth when we see your face and know we cannot live while you are here? This is the boon I choose and I ask from you. Having approached an immortal like you, how can I, subject to old age and death, ever try to rejoice in a long life for the sake of the senses' fleeting pleasures? Dispel this doubt of mine, O Death: Does a person live after death, or does he not?

Nachiketas wants no other boon than the secret of this great mystery."

So, what kind of person is Nachiketas? He's a real spiritual aspirant. Why? Because he doesn't want anything else. He wants to know what happens after death. In other words, does the soul exist? Am I the soul or am I the body that's definitely going to die? He can't be tempted by anything else.

> Yama said, "The joy of the Self, the Atman, ever abides, but not what seems pleasant to the senses. Both these, differing in their purpose, prompt man to action. All is well for those who choose the joy of the Atman, but they miss the goal of life who prefer the pleasant."

Yama is saying that we've got this choice, all the time, in front of us—to choose the pleasures of life, which is quite natural; everybody wants that—or, to try to attain the bliss of the Self, which is very hard, but which will last forever. And the pleasures of the senses, they come and go—we eat something tasty, it's pleasant, and then it's gone. Then again we have to eat something, but we can't do it immediately, because the senses have to recoup—we eat again, and then again it's gone. So it's fleeting. It's just for a moment. Every sensual thing is like that: it comes, it goes. We would like to be able to enjoy nonstop, continuously, day and night. But the very nature of the senses are that they're fleeting—they can give only temporary pleasure, and then they get worn out, they get tired, and then again they must recoup. It's endless. It's like a bottomless pit; we can never fill it up. But the sages say that if one attains the bliss of the Self, the Atman, then that's permanent—that's the essence of bliss. There is always this choice between the pleasant and the good. This is called *preyas* and *sreyas* in Sanskrit.

Yama said, "Perennial joy or passing pleasure. This is the choice one is to make, always. The wise recognize these two, but not the ignorant. The first welcome what leads to abiding joy, though painful at the time; the latter run, goaded by their senses, after what seems immediately pleasurable."

We always are presented with this choice. Not just once in a while; every moment of our life we have this choice, either to run after the pleasurable or to run after the good. And what's good is usually painful at the beginning, but will yield bliss at the end. What's pleasant is very easy to get, but at the end, we have to suffer.

"Well have you renounced these passing pleasures, so dear to the senses, Nachiketas, and turned your back on the ways of the world, which makes mankind forget the goal of life. Far apart are wisdom and ignorance. The first leads to Self-realization; the second makes one more and more estranged from his Real Self. I regard you, Nachiketas, worthy of instruction, for passing pleasures tempt you not at all."

So he's saying to Nachiketas: 'you're a good *sadhak*, and I'm going to teach you'. There's no sense in teaching the science of Self-realization to a person who is a complete sensualist—because they're not concerned about that at all. One should have at least one percent interest in something more than that in order to even hear spiritual talk or read the scriptures. He's got much more than one percent interest, of course.

"It is but a few who hear about the Atma; fewer still dedicate their lives to Its realization. Wonderful is the one who speaks about It; rare are they who make It the supreme goal of their lives. This awakening you have known comes not through logic and scholarship, but from close association with a realized teacher. Wise are you, Nachiketas, because you seek the Self eternal. May we have more seekers like you."

So how do we gain that knowledge? Mainly through the association with a Self-realized Soul.

"Know the Self as the Lord of the chariot."

Now he's instructing him. He praised him for being a fit sadhak; now what is that Self?

"Know the Self as the Lord of the chariot, the body as the chariot itself, the intellect as the charioteer, and the mind as the reins; the senses are the horses; selfish desires are the roads that they travel."

So, we are the charioteer; the body is the chariot; our mind and intellect are the things that hold the reins, and what are the reins connected to? The senses. And where do the senses go? If the road is the sense objects, that's where they go—they go out along the roads. So the roads are the sense objects. Just as the sense of sight sees the objects, the nose smells nice smells, the ears hear nice music—those are like roads. And each one of the senses is like a horse. The mind is holding the reins and deciding which one should go which direction. That's the meaning.

"When one lacks discrimination and his mind is undisciplined, the senses run hither and thither like wild horses."

When one doesn't have any sense of control or discrimination, the senses just go any direction they want. We all might have experienced that. Sometimes we walk through the kitchen, there's something tasty to eat, it's sitting on the counter, and we just go there. We were on our way somewhere else; then our eyes went like that, our nose went like that, our tongue is going to go like that after a few moments. So what's it due to? The reins are loose; the discrimination is gone. We just follow the senses. We do it all the time. The ears, the eyes—everything is like that; the mind just gets pulled whichever way the senses are directed.

> "When one has discrimination and has made the mind one-pointed, then the mind becomes pure and can reach the state of immortality. Those who reach not that state wander from death to death. But those who have discrimination with a still mind and a pure heart reach the journey's end and never again fall into the jaws of death. With a discriminating intellect as charioteer, and a trained mind as reins, they attain the supreme goal of life: to be united with the Lord of Love."

So when we have the reins in our hands, when our senses act the way we want them to rather than us acting the way they want us to, then the mind becomes calm, because the only thing that really agitates the mind is the wandering senses. If the senses get under control, then the mind also becomes calm. In that calm mind then, the Lord of Love, the Paramatman, will be seen reflected in ourself. And that's the state of immortality, when we realize God.

> "Get up! Wake up! Seek the guidance of an illumined teacher and realize the Self."

Now here's a famous saying that most of us might have heard, and this is where it comes from:

> "Sharp like a razor's edge, the sages say, is the path, difficult to traverse."

Spiritual life—the spiritual path—is as sharp as a razor's edge. That's very sharp. In other words, great discipline and precision are needed to succeed in taming the mind.

"The Supreme Self is beyond name and form, beyond the senses, inexhaustible, without beginning, without an end. The Self-existent Lord pierced the senses to turn outwards; thus we look to the world outside and we see not the Atman within us."

The Lord made our senses work like that—our mind goes outwards, it flows out through the senses, so we miss what's inside, which is the Atman, the treasure.

"A sage withdrew his senses from the world, the world of change, and, seeking immortality, he looked within and beheld the deathless Self—the Atman."

So a spiritual person—an aspirant, a sage or a saint, with the desire to escape death—not the death of the body but the feeling that one dies when the body dies—a person who was inspired with that desire, he stilled his senses, looked within for the Self, and then got the vision of the Atman and attained immortality.

Nachiketas said, "After that, how to realize that state?" Yama says:

Yama replied, "The Atman is formless and can never be seen with these two eyes. But He reveals Himself in the heart made pure through meditation and sense restraint. Realizing Him, one is released forever from the cycle of birth and death. When the five senses are stilled, when the mind is stilled, when the intellect is stilled, that is called the highest state by the wise. They say yoga is this complete stillness in which one enters the state of unity, never to become separate again. If one is not established in this state, the sense of unity will come and go. The unitive state cannot be attained through words or thoughts or through the eyes. How can it be attained except through one who is established

31

in this state himself? There are two selves: the separate ego and the indivisible Atman. When one rises above "I" and "me" and "mine", the Atman is revealed as one's real Self. When all desires that surge in the heart are renounced, the mortal becomes immortal. When all the knots that strangle the heart are loosened, the mortal becomes immortal. This sums up the teaching of the Upanishads. The Lord of Love, not larger than a thumb, is ever enshrined in the hearts of all. Draw Him clear out of the physical sheath as one draws the stalk from the grass. Know yourself to be pure and immortal; know yourself to be pure and immortal."

Nachiketas learned from the King of Death the whole discipline of meditation, freeing himself from all sense of separateness. He won immortality in Brahman, the Supreme Being. So blessed is everyone who knows the Self."

The message is very clear: still the mind through spiritual practice; then one can gain the vision of God or the vision of the Self, and that itself is the highest state. Then the individuality subsides into the Ocean of bliss. That's the state of immortality.

Nachiketas is one example of a young person in ancient times that attained Self-realization. There was another young saint, Andal, who was like Amma in many ways.

Andal and Bhagavan Vishnu

During the fifth to ninth centuries in Tamil Nadu near Madurai, many great devotees of Lord Vishnu were born. They came to be known as the "Alwars", which means "the people who are immersed in God-consciousness." One of them was called "Periyalwar", which means "the elder alwar" or "the big alwar", because he had a unique relationship with God. His *ishta devata* (chosen deity) was Krishna, and he loved Krishna like a parent loves a child. So he used to worship baby Krishna, Balakrishna, and received the vision of God in that form.

Periyalwar was well known for his saintliness; even kings knew about him and respected him. His devotion to Lord Vishnu took the form of planting flower gardens and tulasi gardens (tulasi is the basil plant that Vishnu is very fond of). From these flowers, he would make a big garland every day and offer it in the temple in the evening.

One day, he was out in the garden removing weeds from around the tulasi plants, when he found, to his amazement, a little baby girl. She was just lying there under the tulasi plants. He looked around for her parents, but there was nobody to be seen. Then he thought, 'This must be a God-given gift for me.' So he took the little girl home and started raising her as his own daughter. He called her "Goda", which means: "born of the earth." He raised her to be like himself, a devotee of God. Seeing how he was worshipping God every day, immersed in God-consciousness, she also imitated all of his devotional activities.

Goda had a very beautiful attitude towards God, but it was very different from her fathers'. She felt that Lord Vishnu was her beloved. She wanted to get married to Him. She wanted to be the bride of God. You might have heard of bridal mysticism—well, it was sort of like that, where you look upon God as your beloved and you want to marry God, become one with God, unite with God forever. She was having that attitude. It was natural to her, that feeling towards Lord Vishnu.

Periyalwar would make these beautiful garlands and then put them in a basket. After going for his bath in the evening, he'd take them to the temple and offer them to God. When he would go out for his bath, Goda would take the garland, put it on herself, stand in front of a full length mirror, thinking, 'Am

I beautiful enough for Bhagavan?' She was wondering whether Bhagavan was going to marry her or not, and she was just seeing if she looked nice. And then she'd take off the garland and put it back in the basket before her father came.

This was going on for many days. One day, Bhagavan decided He wanted everybody to know about Goda's bhakti, her devotion. So, when Periyalwar took the garland to the temple one evening, Bhagavan made the priest notice one long, black hair in the garland.

The priest said, "What is this? This is a hair! Somebody else was wearing this garland! What kind of nonsense is this? Can you offer this to God? You already gave it to somebody else!!" Periyalwar was shocked. He took the garland and went home. He didn't say anything to Goda; he thought he would to try to catch her in the act.

The next day, he made another garland, kept it in the basket and went out as if going for a bath, but he came around the other side of the house and was standing near the window. Then he saw Goda; she was putting on the garland, standing in front of the mirror and turning herself this side and that side. It wasn't that she was admiring herself; she was just wondering whether Bhagavan would be happy with her as a wife. And then he came rushing in.

"What kind of a sacrilegious thing is this? This is horrible! Who taught you this?" She felt a little shy, so she didn't say anything. That night also, he couldn't go and offer the garland to Bhagavan. He fell asleep. He was very upset. But that night he had a very vivid dream.

Bhagavan Vishnu appeared to him and said, "Periyalwar, don't offer me any garlands except the ones that Goda has worn, because the fragrance of her love adds so much to that garland that I don't like the others anymore. Make sure that she wears the garland first; then only bring it to me."

He was a little surprised, to say the least! He realized that this child was a divine child, the favorite of God. He changed her name after that to Andal, which means: "one who's immersed in the qualities of God." One who's full of God, in other words.

Andal used to go with her friends every morning (especially in the winter time, around December-January)to take a bath in the temple pond, and then they would all go to the Krishna temple and sing songs to Him, asking Him to wake up, asking Him to marry them, and to bless the world with peace. These songs are beautiful and full of devotion. One song of thirty verses called Tiruppavai, even though composed twelve hundred years ago, is sung during that month in all the Vishnu temples in South India and in the houses of all Vaishnavas, Lord Vishnu's devotees.

This was going on for quite a while, and finally, she was a full-grown girl. It was time to get her married. Periyalwar also was getting a little worried, because she seemed almost crazy for God. He thought, like a lot of people think, 'If we get her married, she'll come back down to earth.' So he started looking around for a suitable bridegroom and, when Andal heard about it, just like Amma, she was quite upset.

You might have read in Amma's life story, how many times her parents tried to get her married. It was impossible to get her married. She put obstacles in the way every time.

It was very interesting, some of the things that she did. When they brought one boy to the house to introduce him to her, she stood in the kitchen window with a stone pestle, shaking it as if she was going to beat him to a pulp—this was the prospective bridegroom, and he disappeared like a bullet in the opposite direction. She did other things to discourage her parents from getting her married, until they finally gave up.

They went to an astrologer who told them they were very lucky they didn't succeed in getting this girl married, because whoever the husband would have been, probably he would have died very soon afterwards. She was not intended ever to be married to anybody; she's a divine, yogic personality. This person never met her; just from the horoscope he was able to tell that.

In the same way, Andal didn't want to get married. Periyalwar was a mahatma, not an ordinary person; he was not going to force her. He knew that she was a saint, so he said, "Okay, what do you want? What are you going to do with your life?"

"I want to marry only Bhagavan."

"Which Bhagavan do you want to marry?"

"Vishnu."

"Which Vishnu? There are so many Vishnus."

"What do you mean, there are so many Vishnus?"

"Well, there are so many Vishnu temples."

And he started telling about the different Vishnus—there's this Vishnu, and there's that Vishnu, and finally, when he started talking about Ranganathan in Srirangam—there's a beautiful Vishnu temple in Srirangam—then she blushed. He didn't have to ask her any more. He understood that that's the Vishnu she wanted to marry. That's the Vishnu that she used to see in her dreams and meditations.

So he thought, 'All right, how am I going to get this girl married to a stone? Impossible. Although Vishnu is not a stone, Lord Sri Ranganatha is definitely in the form of a stone. How am I going to get my flesh daughter married to a stone God?' He was in a fix. That night, he also had a dream in which Ranganatha said, "Don't worry about it, I'll arrange everything."

So, Periyalwar called all his relatives, they got Andal into a palanquin, and started taking her to the temple in Sri Rangam. In the meantime, Sri Ranganatha appeared to the priests there and said, "My beloved is coming, my bride is coming. Get ready for the marriage ceremony."

When everybody met near the temple, the priests welcomed her with all honors as if she was the beloved of God. Still, no one had any idea what was going to happen, how this marriage was going to take place. They must have thought: 'okay, at the most we make Andal go into the temple, we do some rituals and it will be over and she'll go back home with her father, she'll be happy for the rest of her life, she married God.' That's what they were thinking, naturally. But that's not what happened.

They went into the temple, and, when Andal saw Sri Ranganatha—she had never seen that image of God—tears welled up and she grew effulgent. As if in a trance, she walked up to the image in the temple, stood next to it and started to glow more and more until she just vanished into light.

Everybody standing there was in shock. Especially Periyalwar who had lost his daughter. But everything became clear to him then; he realized that she was the Divine Mother Herself.

This has happened to one other lady saint—Mirabai. Mirabai also was mad for Krishna, and this is exactly the same way that she ended her life. She went into a Krishna temple in Dwaraka, went up to the image and merged in light. There's no samadhi, there's no tomb, of Mirabai. Both of these lady mahatmas disappeared just like that. There's a nice poem written by a Bengali devotee, in honor of Andal. After he read Andal's story, he wrote this little poem.

> Like some blessed fountain from the very core of your
> rich heart, O Saint, did you outpour your crystal holy
> love and ecstasy to God,

O bird with wings outspread in glee, adoration's summit did you overpeer, and earth and sky were glad and evermore drink deep your song's ambrosial melody.

Your love was not of earth, no woman's soul for mortal love craved with such a yearning.
So you did wed the great God Himself,

O goal beyond our ken, beyond our dim discerning, and soul to soul, like sunbeam into the sun, did you vanish away, O mystic One.

Faith in Amma

Perfect Faith is Self-realization

Amma says—and we know it, we're all spiritually minded—that the goal of human life is God-realization; that the thirst we have for happiness, which never subsides whatever we may do, can be satisfied only in the bliss of God-realization. Because the thirst is infinite, only something that's infinite can satisfy it. So nothing we do that is finite, that gives a finite pleasure, can yield the satisfaction we're seeking. And we can never turn off that thirst. We can never say, "Hey, I've had enough of this! I'm just going to be happy." You can't just be happy unless you merge into God, or unless you realize your real Self.

For that to be possible, Amma says we need perfect faith. In fact, perfect faith is Self-realization or God-realization. That's a rather cryptic statement. What does she mean by that? At present, for us, the world and the body are real. They're the only reality that exists. And God or the *Atman*, the Self, doesn't exist at all. It seems to be just an abstraction. People use the word God in many ways, and that's about the only reality of God there is—just as a word, not as an experience. That's called *Maya*, when we feel like that, that God isn't real and the Atman doesn't exist and the body, the personality, the world is real, that means we're under the influence of Maya, the cosmic illusion. Because of that, we don't feel the infinite happiness of God-realization.

What Amma says is, we have to cultivate just the opposite, that God alone exists, that only the Atman is real, that the body, the personality, the world are unreal and just dreams in the cosmic existence, in Pure Consciousness. Not only do we need to think like that, and cultivate that, but we have to live by it, which is even more difficult. In fact, that's the main difficulty in spiritual life. Spiritual life doesn't mean to just do our mantra a hundred and eight times morning and evening, go to the temple, offer a puja, meditate, go to the holy places, visit Amma. No. That's not everything in spiritual life. Real spiritual life means to live by faith, to live by the faith that God alone exists and only the Atman is real. Everything else is a dream. That's real spirituality, that's real religion, that's dharma, that's *tapas* (austerity), that's everything in spiritual life.

The Atheist Who Fell Off a Cliff

Many of you must have heard this story, but it's very to the point. It's a very funny story about the atheist who was running and fell off a cliff. As he was falling down, he caught hold of a branch that was sticking out of the side of the mountain. He was clinging to that and about one thousand feet below was an abyss he was about to fall into. He'd be crushed, shattered to pieces. So, as he was holding on, he was getting weaker and weaker, and couldn't hold on anymore. He was trying his level best to find some way out of this predicament. Finally, an idea occurred to him: 'God!' Until then he didn't care about God. He never thought about God. And he thought: 'God!' So he shouted out, "Oh, God!"

No answer. So he thought, 'What can I lose? Let me try one more time. Maybe He didn't hear me. "Oh God! If You'll just save me, I'll believe in You for the rest of my life. I'll spread Your glory all over the world!"

No answer. Silence.

"Oh, God, don't You hear me? Really, if You save me, I'll believe in You."

Silence. After a moment, a tremendous thundering voice came out of the valley, "All of you say like that when you're in trouble."

The man was thrilled. "No, no, God. I'm different! I'll do whatever You tell me. Just save me and I'll spread Your name all over the world!"

"All right, let go of that branch."

"What? Do You think I'm crazy?!"

That was his faith; that much faith only! Even when he heard the voice of God, he still couldn't obey that. He had too much faith in the material world.

This is the crux of the problem. Amma is saying, "Have faith in God. Have faith in a God-realized Guru. Everything will be all right. That's the magic key to becoming perfect, to becoming happy." But when it comes to tackling the practical problems with faith in God, somehow our faith goes down the drain completely and we're back in the world. We're all right as long as we're singing *bhajans* or we're in Amma's lap. Then it all just evaporates if there's a problem.

In the *Bhagavad Gita* there's great stress laid on faith in the sense that, as per our faith, that is exactly what we are. In the eyes of God, or a God-realized Soul, we could say that our level is determined by our intensity or our degree of faith. Lord Krishna says in the Gita,

> "The faith of each one is in accordance with his nature.
> The man is made up of his faith. As a man's faith is,
> so is he."
>
> —Ch. 17, v. 3

So that's what we are. What we have faith in, how much faith we have, that's our stage in spiritual evolution. All of us have faith in something always, because, as we are going to read now in Amma's words, we can't exist without some kind of faith. We would just cease to be. Why?

Faith is Necessary for God-realization

One person asked Amma: "Isn't it blind faith to say that there is a God?"

In fact, Amma is saying, there is no such thing as blind faith; all faith is blind faith. Why?

"Children, everyone lives by faith."

These are Amma's words.

"Having the faith that there's nothing harmful in front of us, we take each step. We do not place our foot down if we think a poisonous snake may be in front of us. We eat food from restaurants because we believe that there is no danger in doing so. But there are people dying from food poisoning, aren't there? Life itself would become impossible if we did not believe blindly.

"When we get into a bus, we blindly believe in the driver even though he is a complete stranger. He might have even caused several accidents. How many bus and car accidents occur every day? Even then, what makes us travel in a bus or car again? Faith, is it not? What about traveling in an airplane? Usually, not even one person will escape alive in a plane crash, yet we believe that the pilot will take us safely to our destination.

"Take the case of a business man. What makes him start a business? Isn't it faith that he will be able to make some profit out of it? What guarantee is there that all these things will happen as we expect? None at all. So why do we continue to do everything that we do? Faith!"

Amma differentiates between faith in worldly things and faith in God, spirituality, or God-realized people.

> "Real faith, however, is different from the aforesaid ordinary faith. Faith should be born of meaningful principles. Only then can it be called faith. It was through such faith that our ancestors lived abiding in God. None of them believed blindly."

So what does she mean here? That they didn't just believe in God; they experienced God.

> "Those who have seen God directly become witnesses to His existence. Their testimony does not become invalid simply because we have not seen Him. Those who have seen Him prescribe the way for others to see Him. It is not right to reject their testimony without following their advice on a trial basis, is it? Is it not a kind of blind faith to reject something without experimentation?"

Some sceptics say that, just because the rishis or a mahatma say that they have seen God and that I should also try to see God by following their instructions, why should I believe that? How do I know that they saw God? What is the proof? To question like that is like saying that we don't believe our grandfather when he says that he saw his grandfather. This cannot be proven, but we do accept his word for it. In the same way, we should accept the authority of great people or sages when they say that God does exist, that they saw God, and that there is a way to realize God. Faith in a God-realized person or Master is very essential. That's the starting point for God-realization.

> "To go to an unknown place, one must put one's faith in a guide. When such is the case for reaching a physical destination, what could be the objection to placing one's

faith in a Realized Soul in order to reach the supremely subtle and mysterious Reality?"

Be Like a Child

Faith is necessary for God-realization, but it doesn't stop there. Faith is necessary for a quality life. In fact, that's the secret to developing a perfect life, through faith in God or faith in a Guru. Amma continues to explain why that's so:

"Faith in God gives one the mental strength needed to confront the problems of life. Faith in the existence of God is a protective force. It makes one feel safe and protected from all the evil influences of the world. To have faith in the existence of a Supreme Power and to live accordingly is what's called religion. When we become religious, morality arises, which in turn will help to keep us away from malevolent influences. We won't drink, we won't smoke, we'll stop wasting our energy through gossip and unnecessary talk. Morality, or purity of character, is a stepping-stone to spirituality.

"Faith brings about these different stepping-stones of real spirituality, not to mention the benefit of keeping the mind peaceful and strong in the midst of the problems of life. We will also develop qualities like love, compassion, patience, mental equipoise and other positive traits. These will help us to love and serve everyone equally. Religion is faith. When there is faith, there's harmony, unity and love. A non-believer always doubts. He does not believe in unity or in love. He likes to cut and divide. Everything is food for his intellect. He cannot be at peace. He's restless. He always questions, therefore, the foundation of his entire life is unstable and scattered due to his lack of faith in a higher principle."

We read the *Bhagavatam, Ramayana, Mahabharata*, and other ancient stories that were written by the sages thousands of years ago. The rishis say that we shouldn't read these things books with our intellect. We need not try to understand the intended or inner meaning of the stories. We should read them like children read children's stories, because that will purify our mind and make us innocent like a child. Whenever Amma comes here, she stresses again and again that we are too much in the head. That's why we're not happy, because our heart is dry. Thinking, understanding, and knowing are intellect-based. We are lacking in feelings. We hardly ever use them.

There's nothing wrong with the intellect, we do need it, but that's not where the primary center of our life should be. That should be the heart. That's where God resides. That's where the Atman shines. That is where we feel. The intellect is just our assistant and should follow the heart's commands.

Children live in the heart. Their intellects are not yet developed. What did Christ say? "Truly, I tell you, unless you change and become like little children, you will never enter the kingdom of heaven." The kingdom of heaven is a spiritual state of innocence experienced by a pure mind. All the sages have said the same thing.

When God Lives in You

"A person who is endowed with real faith will be steadfast. A person who has religion can find peace."

We should remember that when Amma uses the word religion, she doesn't mean just having a religion or believing in a religion. She means that, even if one doesn't have any official religion, having faith in God or in spiritual principles or a Divine Being means a person is leading a religious life. And she says here also, "A person with faith believes in unity, love and peace—not in division and disharmony." Amma is not talking about religion in the narrow sense but in the broadest sense.

"Due to the lack of faith in a Supreme Power, non-believers will not have anything to hold onto and surrender to fully when adverse circumstances arise. As far as a believer is concerned, God is the Supreme Being. God is an experience. God lives in us. Desireless love, compassion, forbearance, renunciation and qualities like these will manifest in us through belief in a Supreme Being."

This is a beautiful statement. Amma is saying that, when we express these qualities such as desireless love, which is love towards anyone without wanting anything in return, or compassion, patience, or self-sacrifice, what happens is that at that moment God shines in us. God is already in us, but God starts to shine through us, God's presence starts to manifest in us. We start to experience the benefit of that kind of life. Even if it is just for a moment, we will feel a kind of refined happiness, not the happiness of getting and enjoying and taking, but the subtle happiness of the expansion or blossoming of the heart. That is gained through developing these principles or qualities of spirituality.

"If a non-believer has any of these qualities in him, he will get all the benefits of a believer. What I mean by a believer is not someone who has faith in a God or a Goddess, but someone who gives value to higher principles for which he is willing to sacrifice everything. If these qualities serve as the principles by which the non-believer lives his life, he'll be equal to a believer. On the other hand, if those qualities are only on the outside, and they're shallow and not deep, a person will not have the benefits of a true believer. Often non-believers like to talk but they do not put their words into practice.

They are shallow and talk only to put on an impressive show. They do not have anything to hold onto. They lack the faith in the supreme Governor of the Universe to save them from the problems of life."

Story of Job

There's a beautiful story in the Old Testament. It's the story of Job. Many of us are familiar with the story of Job, but it's worth repeating.

Job was a very virtuous person. He was very, very rich. In fact, he was the richest man in the place that he was living. He had thousands of cattle, thousands of sheep, tens of thousands of camels, and he was having plenty of money and land. He had ten children also.

One day, there was a meeting going on in one of the higher worlds. The Lord was sitting there, and many of the minor gods came, as well as demonic beings—the chief amongst them being Satan, as he is known in the Bible. Of course, in the Hindu tradition, there is no supreme demon, but there are plenty of very bad ones. He was probably one such. Perhaps Satan is the head of some of the demonic hoards, the mafia of the other world. He probably doesn't have pointy ears and a pointy tail, but for sure he's pretty horrible to see.

God asked him, "Satan, where were you today? Anything special going on?"

Satan replied, "I was down on the Earth. I was just traveling around to see if there was any mischief I could do."

"Did you see my servant, Job? He's my best servant. In fact, he's the best man on the Earth. Did you see him there?"

"I saw him. What's so great about him? You pay him very well. Why shouldn't he worship You? You gave him so much of property and camels and children. He has everything. Why shouldn't he worship You? If You really want to prove his worth, take away all his wealth."

"All right. Go and do whatever you like to him, but don't hurt him physically."

So Satan went back down to Earth. And what happened?

Next day, Job was sitting in his house. He got the news: the cattle herd was struck by lightning, they were all destroyed; the sheep were stolen away by the neighboring tribes; the camels died of poisoned water. Not only that; as if that was not bad enough, all the children were in one of the brother's houses when a tornado came, knocked over the house, and everybody was killed.

So what did Job say? What would we have said, if that had happened to us? Probably not what he said!

He said, "Naked I came out of my mother's womb, and naked shall I return: the Lord has given, and the Lord has taken away; blessed be the name of the Lord." This was Job's attitude. This is why God considered him His greatest devotee.

The next day, Satan came to talk to God again. God asked him, "Well, what happened? Did you see Job? What did you do?"

"Yeah, I saw him. He's pretty good even though You destroyed all his stuff. But that was only his possessions. Just try and hurt his body and You'll see what a great devotee he is! I bet he'll curse You.

"Okay, you can go and do whatever you like, but don't kill him."

So Satan went down and afflicted Job with boils. His whole body from top to bottom was covered with boils. Well, we know how painful it is if we have only one little boil somewhere. He was covered with boils. They started to burst; they were oozing pus. Worms started crawling in the wounds. He was in really bad shape and this continued for months and months. If we're suffering like that for months and months and months, what will happen? Our faith will start to get a little weak.

Some friends came to Job to comfort him. They heard that he had lost everything. He'd lost all his wealth, lost all his property, lost his children. He had nothing. Only his wife was there, and the house he was living in, and he was deathly sick. So they tried to comfort him but to no avail. Finally, they said, "You must have done a lot of bad things to have to suffer like this."

It's natural, when we see somebody suffering, we think like that: 'They did a lot of bad karma, so they're suffering like this.'

But in the Bible, in those days they didn't believe in the theory of past lives. We're born once and after we die, that's it. We don't get born again. So Job was thinking, 'What did I do in this life? I didn't do anything wrong. Why are they accusing me like this?"

The friends said, "If you just repent for all the bad things you did, if you just admit it before God, everything will be all right. It'll all disappear."

Job thought, 'I didn't do anything wrong. Why are they talking like this? Are you guys the only ones that know something? Am I so stupid? I'll teach you a few things about the ways of God. You think you're so wise, you know it all!'

Then he started to complain to God. This is very interesting because, those of us who've suffered a lot also may do a similar thing. It happens to come out like this, if our faith isn't strong. So what does Job say?

"O God, am I some kind of monster that You torture me like this? You've taken away my family and my wealth and You've turned me into skin and bones because of my so-called evil deeds. I was living quietly until You broke me apart. You have taken me by the neck and dashed me to pieces. And then hung me up as Your target with Your archers surrounding me letting their arrows fly.

"Yet, I'm innocent! You don't even let me sleep peacefully, but give me nightmares! Must You test me every moment of the day? Did I hurt You, the All-powerful? And, if You accuse me of doing wrong, what can I say? I can't even defend myself against Your accusations because You are not a man like me. And we could not discuss the matter fairly, with there being no possibility of having an umpire between us.

"Don't just torture me! Tell me why You are doing it. You have made me and You are destroying me. It is better that I die."

And to his friends he said, "What miserable comforters all of you are! What have I said that makes you speak so endlessly? Are you the only ones that know anything? Do you have a monopoly on wisdom? Don't I know anything? Stop accusing me of wicked things! I know what's right and I know what's wrong! "

Well, he didn't quite curse God, but he was about to— he was just on the verge of doing it.

"Why are You treating me like this? You created me, and if You would at least tell me why I am suffering like this, I wouldn't mind so much. But what's the use of suffering and not knowing why you're suffering? And what's the benefit of all this?"

This is what happens to all of us. These are the doubts that come up in our minds when our faith gets weak.

Job's ego, his arrogance, his pride, all the bad qualities that are inside everybody, came up under the force of suffering which is one of the reasons that suffering comes—so that all of that stuff can come out. Amma says that whatever is inside has to come out. Then, when it comes out, if we know how to handle it properly, if we understand what is happening and then decide, 'I'm not going to let this take hold of me, I'm not going to let it happen again,' then we are rid of it. Our mind becomes clear like a dirty ink bottle that has been washed out until it is clean. When all the inner rubbish that is hiding in our subconscious mind comes out through the force of suffering, then the peaceful presence of God can shine forth.

At last, when all the wind had blown out of the sails of his ego, God spoke saying, "Why are you using your ignorance to deny My wisdom? All these ignorant arguments you are giving imply that I don't know what I'm doing with you. What do you know? Now, get ready to fight, for I'm going to demand some answers from you, and you must reply.

"Where were you when I laid the foundations of the Earth? Do you know how the Earth's dimensions were determined and who did the surveying? Do you know who was the engineer? Who decreed the boundaries for the oceans? Has the location of the gate of death been revealed to you? Who dug the valleys and who made the sun? Who laid down the path for lightning and the rain? Who gives intuition and instinct? Who provides for the young of animals?

"Do you still want to argue with Me? Do you, God's critic, have the answers?"

What would we have said if we heard that voice? If we had learned our lessons, we would say exactly what Job says, "I'm nothing. How could I ever find the answers? I lay my hand upon my mouth in silence. I've already said too much."

God didn't stop. He saw there was still some ego in Job, so He said, "Stand up like a man and fight! Let Me ask you some more questions. Are you going to discredit My justice and condemn Me without a battle?"

"I'm sorry, Lord, I know nothing. In my pain I uttered many unbecoming things. Have mercy on me, Your child."

God was pleased. Job became truly humble. He became like a child. That is the purpose of difficulties. That's the purpose of suffering. It's just to make us humble like a child so that faith can blossom, so we can feel the bliss of the Divine Presence.

Then God blessed him so that all his land and all the animals should be restored. He had another ten children after that and he lived for one-hundred and forty years. He even saw his great-great-grandchildren, and then died a peaceful death.

If we're having sufferings—and everybody has sufferings, there's nobody who doesn't suffer in some way or other at some time or other—we shouldn't curse God or curse our Guru, or curse Amma. We should remember that the purpose of suffering is to purify us, to make us humble so that we can get faith and enjoy the bliss of God-realization.

In the Gita, one of the last things Krishna says is,

> "The man who hears this teaching, full of faith and free from malice, even he, liberated, shall attain to the happy worlds of the righteous."

—Ch. 18, v. 71

With full faith, if we follow the path of faith, then we'll attain the divine world and merge into God.

Developing Willpower

THIS IS NEW YEAR'S DAY. ONE NICE TRADITION in the West on New Year's Day is to make New Year's resolutions. We need not think it's just a Western tradition. In fact, it's a spiritual tradition. It's not something unique to the Western world on New Year's Day. All of us, every day, are supposed to review what's good and what's bad in our mind; what's taking us forward and what's taking us backwards. Then, when we go to sleep at night, we should make the resolve that tomorrow we'll be better. And that when we get up in the morning, we should think, "Okay, today I'll conquer my weaknesses and cultivate good qualities."

On New Year's Eve, everyone sort of throws away all their bad habits and decides that from the next day onwards they will improve themselves. But even though we decide that we're going to get rid of our negative tendencies, our *vasanas*, we find that our resolutions don't last very long. That's usually the case with New Year's resolutions. Why don't they last very long? There are a number of reasons, and that's what we are going to talk about today.

Vasanas are Like a Bear

The main reason is that our willpower is not very strong. Our mind is weak. Willpower means to be able to put into practice our good intentions. But we're not usually able to do this. Why? Because our mind easily gets distracted. This is what spiritual practice is for. We may want to get rid of a bad habit, but the bad habit doesn't want to leave us.

Once, two poor sadhus were swimming across a river when they saw something come floating by. One of the sadhus thought, 'It's a blanket. Oh great! I can get a blanket. I didn't have one until now.' He caught hold of it, but both he and the "blanket" keep floating down the river.

The other sadhu said, "Come on! We have to cross the river. Let go of that thing!" Well, that thing which he thought was a blanket was actually a bear. So the other man shouted to his friend, "I want to let go of it, but it's not letting go of me!"

Vasanas are just like this. We want to let go of them, we want them to go away, but they're not letting go of us, because we've been cultivating them for many years, we've been feeding them and fondling them and kissing them, and so they don't want to go so easily.

Here is one suggestion as to how to get rid of the vasanas. When they come up, mercilessly beat them. Of course, not with a stick or anything like that, because they're immaterial, they're subtle, they're in the mind.

A person who has a monkey and is always fondling, kissing, and hugging it, doesn't realize that it is an animal and may bite him one day. He has a friend who comes to him and says, "Don't you know you may get bit? You shouldn't fondle the monkey like that."

Taking this advice to heart, this person tells the monkey the next time it comes, "No! No! Sorry, you can't jump on me! You can't kiss me anymore!"

The monkey just jumps on him anyhow because he doesn't understand. Our vasanas are like that. We may make a decision: 'I'm not going to do this thing, or I'm not going to talk like that or I'm not going to look over there, or I'm not going to eat this.'

We've made the decision, but the vasanas don't know anything about it. So then when the cake comes, or the person that we don't like comes, we eat the thing, or we say the thing impulsively, because we did it so many times, because vasanas don't know, they're just habits. What we have to do is to hit it hard. If we don't want the monkey to jump on us, you may have to hit it. It's not cruel. We have to teach it a lesson. And, if it still jumps on us, we have to hit it again. So, some bad habits—we have to be merciless about routing them out. They will come again and again until they get the idea, and then they'll stay away.

One reason why we can't get strength of mind is that we're not very serious about it. Unless we're very serious about culturing our mind, it will be very difficult to conquer the mind. It's a full time job. We can't go one step forward and ten steps backwards and expect to get the mind to attain concentration and peace. And a mind that's cultured, a mind that's strong, is a mind that's peaceful and happy. So we have to have the requisite seriousness for that. That's why people make New Year's resolutions and don't succeed, because they're not serious about it. It's just today they feel like that, but not tomorrow or the day afterwards.

For a spiritual person, it has to be not just today and tomorrow and the day afterwards. Every minute until the last breath, we have to be trying to purify the mind. This is what it's all about. Purity of mind. Purity of mind means the power to control the mind and make it do what we want rather than having it do what it likes. It means to be able to not think, to exist with a thought-free mind, just awareness, peaceful awareness without thoughts. We can think if we want to, but we don't have to helplessly think.

Feeling the Burden of the Ego

Unless we reach a certain state where we feel, "What a burden my mind is, and all these bad habits—how heavy they are! What a source of suffering they are to me," that requisite seriousness won't come. We have to reach the point where we feel that the ego is such a burden. Not the pure ego—the pure ego's okay. The pure ego will help us, but the negative ego, the ego full of negative qualities, must go. "Again, I said like that! Again, I did like this!" When we feel the suffering caused by our impulsive actions, we will become serious.

Amma has something to say about that:

> "If the goal is to realize the Supreme Being, you should become completely egoless. That requires self-effort. The *sadhak* himself must pray sincerely for the removal of his negative tendencies. He should work hard. This prayer is not to achieve anything, or to fulfill any desire. It is to go beyond all achievements. It's to transcend all desires. It is an intense longing of the sadhak to return to his original and real abode. He feels and becomes aware of the burden of his own ego and this feeling creates a strong urge to unburden its heaviness. It is this urge that expresses itself as prayer. Removal of the ego cannot be attained through the prayers of another limited soul. It takes self-effort and the guidance of a perfect Master."

Sometimes people say, "Please pray for me." Amma's saying that prayers done for others are effective for everything except this—for getting rid of the ego. We can pray for others' health and others' wealth or others' well-being, but when it comes to removing the ego, each one has to do it himself. Nobody except the Guru can do it.

> "So the prayers of another limited soul will not help that. Working on the ego or emptying the mind becomes easier in the presence of a Divine Master. Even though Amma has said that somebody else's prayer cannot help remove another person's ego, a Realized Guru's mere thought, look or touch can bring about a tremendous

transformation in the disciple. If he so wishes, a real Guru can even bestow Self-realization on the disciple or devotee. He can do anything he likes. His will is one with God's will. Praying for the fulfillment of petty desires is being stuck to your mind and all its attachments and aversions. Not only that; it is adding more to the existing vasanas."

We're talking about habits, vasanas—bad habits particularly. When we use prayer as a means to control our mind or as a means to purify our mind, we should pray for the highest thing, not for lesser things, because lesser things just increase our desires, our vasanas. It's amounting to praying to God to increase our bondage and our suffering when we pray for anything less than God-realization. If we make that choice, it's all right, there's nothing wrong with it. But for one whose goal is to realize the bliss of God, if one feels that that's the ultimate, then one has to pray only for that.

"New desires, new worlds are created. Along with that, you lengthen the chain of your anger, lust, greed, jealousy, delusion, and all other negative traits. Each desire brings with it those negative emotions. Unfulfilled desires result in anger. In contrast to that, when one prays for purification for the purpose of creating Self-realization, or awareness of the Self, the vasanas are destroyed. Such prayer will totally change your outlook toward life. The old person dies and a new one is born. However, praying for the fulfillment of petty desires does not involve any change in one's personality. The person who prays in this way remains the same. His attitude remains unchanged."

Many people say, "I've been praying to God for so many years and still I'm not making any spiritual progress. I go to the church every week, every Sunday."

Why? Why don't they make any progress? One reason is that their mind is still occupied with, as Amma says, "petty desires," not the highest desire for God.

Control of the mind, either through prayer or other means, is not just for us, not just for devotees, not just for spiritual people. It's for everybody. Because if we can't control our mind, there's no way to succeed. It will always be distracted by various things, and the goal that we set won't be possible to reach.

Steps of Yoga

Many of us might have heard of the *Yoga Sutras,* the most authoritative text on meditation. It was written about two thousand of years ago by a great sage named Patanjali. The very first verse says, "yogascitta vritti nirodhah" which means, "Yoga is control of the modifications of the mind." That's the real meaning of yoga. Today, the meaning of yoga has just become doing yogic postures. But the real purpose of the postures and all the branches of yoga is to control the waves of the mind, to bring the mind to a standstill, to make the mind perfectly peaceful. In the yogic system of controlling the mind, there are steps. Many of us are aware of what those steps are, but today I thought we'd talk at least a little about them. We'll go into more detail some other day.

If we want to attain a certain goal, we have to apply the requisite means. That principle applies just as stringently to attaining peace of mind. It can't be done haphazardly. It has to be done according to science. The science of yoga says that the first steps in that process are called *yama* and *niyama*. It means restraint. The restraints are the yamas. The observances are the niyamas. It's like the do's and the don'ts of spiritual life. Most people meditate, they read spiritual books, and they do a lot of things, but they neglect the yamas and the niyamas. It's like neglecting the foundation and then building a house on sand. I don't know how many people I've heard come to Amma and say, "Amma, I've been meditating thirty-five years, but I don't have any experience!" Why? Because the foundation was neglected. Just meditating is not enough. Just doing bhajans is not enough. The foundation—the yamas and the niyamas—have to be attended to, and if they're attended to, if these basic things are done properly, the next step automatically comes. Meditation will come automatically. No separate effort has to be made for that. That's not to say that we shouldn't meditate. We should meditate but, at the same time, we shouldn't neglect the basics, the foundation.

What are the yamas?

Ahimsa: non-injury

Satya: truthfulness

Asteya: abstention from stealing

Brahmacharya: continence

Aparigraha: abstinence from avariciousness

In brief, non-injury means to not hurt any living thing through thought, word or deed. Just imagine, if we can perfect ourselves in even this one discipline, how pure our mind will be; how effectively our vasanas will be removed!

Satya means truthfulness. Truthfulness doesn't mean just not telling lies. Truthfulness is speech that will help us and others move towards the truth. If it's an unpleasant truth, the scriptures say it shouldn't be told. Just because we are being truthful, we shouldn't go and tell people their faults. That's a very common thing that people do. It is not to be done because of the painful reaction it causes; in other words, it is harmful. So we shouldn't tell an unpleasant truth. It's better to keep silent than to create waves like that.

Some people ask, "Shouldn't I tell the truth? Shouldn't I tell them that they're doing something wrong?" No, we don't tell unless asked. If we're the person who's asked, if that person has confidence in us, then we can tell them because then it won't create a negative wave in them. It won't make them angry. Otherwise it's none of our business. We need too mind our own business!

Asteya is abstention from stealing, meaning not even to think, 'I'd like that!' when it belongs to somebody else, much less actually taking it. If it's nice and we want it, then go out and get one. We don't take somebody else's.

Brahmacharya is sexual continence. Continence means that physically, mentally, and verbally one's mind lives in God, not in sexual matters. This includes even the subtlest movements of the mind and senses.

Aparigraha is abstinence from avariciousness. What's necessary for me? I want only that much. I don't want any more than that because more than that entails work and strain and an unnecessary waste of life. Another way of saying it is to follow the way of simplicity.

We may feel, after following these rules for a while, "That's enough. I've reached a good stage and now I'm happy." In all probability, it may not be enough. The same Yoga Sutras tell us when we've had enough. For example, when we're perfect in non-injury, then all beings that come near us will cease to be hostile. There are many stories about this. Yogis that were walking through the forest or living in a cave with snakes suffered no harm from ferocious animals because their minds were always established in non-injury, and they never had a feeling of injuring another; so other beings also became harmless in front of them.

One day, some of us were trying to move the ashram cows to another part of the pasture. Normally, the cows ignored our presence. We could even be two or three feet away from them and they would go about their business. But this day, I came out of the house with a stick. The cows were about a hundred yards away from me. As soon as they saw me, they started running. They couldn't have seen that stick. I was just dragging it along behind me. They seemed to know that I had the idea in my mind: 'I'm going to chase them. If they don't cooperate, I may have to hit them.' They intuitively knew that. Their power of intuition is much more than ours. Perhaps because they don't speak, their energy doesn't dissipate like ours. They depend on their intuition for their survival.

Many living beings sense when they are being threatened. If we're really established in harmlessness, all living beings should become harmless before us.

Then there's truthfulness. When we don't tell lies or exaggerate, and our speech is always beneficial, then a power develops which will cause anything we say to come true. Amma may say, "Don't worry. You'll become better." If she says so, then you will become better. We can't say when that will happen, but it definitely will happen.

Non-stealing is a very interesting one. It says in the scriptures that, "One who's established in non-stealing, to such a one, gems come." The word is *ratna*, gems. Strange, no? What is a sannyasi, a monk, going to do with gems? But the meaning of gems is not precious stones. When a person is established in non-stealing, they have such a look of innocence, such a look of disinterestedness and detachment that other people are inspired with trust toward them. Then they feel inclined to give all the best things to such a person, either to share with them or to entrust with them. This is because they feel intuitively that this person is not going to steal; he is detached. Then all the best things come to such a person.

When one is perfect in continence, when one doesn't have even a sexual thought, what happens? One develops spiritual

energy, spiritual power. When a person has the power of continence called *virya*, then when they talk to you, their words pierce
your heart. This does not happen because of the person's style of
speaking or feeling behind their words. It's the spiritual energy
they've developed through brahmacharya, or continence. People
won't even know why they feel that way. We will feel sublimated.
Their speech will be a real *satsang*, and while listening, we'll forget everything and live in a spiritual world. Of course, to fully
experience that, we should also have receptivity.

Non-covetousness: this is also very interesting. Patanjali says
that, when we have become perfect in non-covetousness, we get
a particular *siddhi* (a mystic power). Mystic powers are latent in
everybody. They are the powers of a concentrated mind. Normally, our mind is scattered; we can't concentrate, and so those
powers don't manifest. Sunlight cannot burn a paper, but if it is
concentrated through a magnifying glass, it can. So, when we
develop the quality of non-covetousness, when we don't want
anything except the minimum for ourself, what happens is that we
become detached from the world. We don't care about anything.
And when we become detached from the world, the next thing
is we become detached from our own body. Just the minimum
is enough—a place to live, something to eat, a place to sleep—the
minimum. And when you become truly detached from the body,
spiritual knowledge starts to shine. Patanjali says the knowledge
of the past and future dawns on the person who is established
in non-covetousness. Why? Because they're not concerned even
with the present anymore. They're detached.

These are the qualities of yamas. Then there's the niyamas:

Saucha—cleanliness. Cleanliness means both physical cleanliness and inner purity of mind.

Santosha—contentment. The feeling that I have enough.
Why should I feel restless about getting this and that? Where is

the end to the craving for more and more? Don't I have enough? Feeling like this is called santosha.

All these qualities are conducive to controlling the mind, making it peaceful.

Tapas—austerity. Nowadays, the word tapas is used to mean suffering, "Oh, what a tapas that was!" But it doesn't mean suffering. On the other hand, it means the capacity to bear suffering. It means that, when it's cold or hot, we will not get distressed and exclaim, "It's so cold! It's so hot! I can't bear it." Or, "What a terrible headache! I feel like dying." To stay even-minded amongst all these opposites, the *dvandas*, is called tapas. To maintain our cool under all circumstances, to keep an even mind, is tapas.

Svadhyaya is the study of the scriptures, the writings of the sages. Study of the scriptures doesn't mean reading spiritual books that any so-called spiritual person has written. If we go to any bookstore, we'll find hundreds, even thousands of them. Nowadays, everybody writes spiritual books, and everybody reads spiritual books. But that's not what svadhyaya is. Svadhyaya is reading the books written by rishis, books written by Realized Souls, not just anybody who knows something about spiritual matters. The power of the words of a Realized person, ancient or modern, is very strong and has the capability to purify our minds.

Crying to God is Meditation

The last thing is *Ishwara pranidhana,* which means devotion to God. All the items before this are very good. We should do them. But we're just ordinary human beings. It's very difficult to do everything we're talking about. So Amma says, well, don't worry, there's a way out. That's also not easy but it's not so complicated as the other ones. That is *ishwara bhakti,* or devotion to God. This is the way to control the mind, to get rid of the vasanas. What does Mother say about it?

"One of the brahmacharis asked Amma, 'Amma, this afternoon you instructed a young man just to pray and cry to God. Is that enough to know God?'

"Yes," Amma said, "if performed with all one's heart! Son, don't think that spiritual practice is only sitting in the lotus posture meditating or repeating a mantra. Of course, those two are ways and techniques to remember God and to know the Self. They certainly will help to train and tame the naturally restless body and mind; but it's wrong to think that these practices alone are the way. Take, for example, the gopis of Vrindavan, or Mirabai. What was their sadhana? How did they become Krishnamayis? (Krishnamayi means one who is full of Krishna.) Was it from long hours sitting in meditation?" Were the gopis doing that? Was there time? The gopis were householders. No. But of course, they did meditate. They did constant and intense meditation but not sitting with crossed legs. Devotees like the gopis and Mirabai constantly remembered the glories of God cherishing His form within themselves, irrespective of time or place. They just cried and cried until their tears washed away their entire mind stuff, until all their thoughts were gone.

"Children, when we cry, we can forget everything effortlessly. Crying helps us to stop brooding on the past and dreaming about the future. It helps us to be in the present with the Lord and His leela. Suppose someone is very dear to us and they die: say our mother, or father, our husband or our wife, a son or a daughter. We'll lament thinking of him or her, won't we? We forget everything else. At that moment, nothing else comes to mind except the sweet memories of the departed one.

We'll have no other interest than thinking about that person. Our minds become fully focused. Children, crying has the power to make the mind completely one-pointed. Why do we meditate? To get concentration. So the best way to get concentration is by crying to God. That is a very powerful way of remembering God and that in fact is meditation.

"That is what great devotees like the gopis and Mirabai did. See how selflessly Mirabai prayed, "Oh, Mira's Giridhari, it doesn't matter if you love me, but Lord, please, don't take away my right to love You!" They prayed and cried until their whole being was transformed into a state of constant prayer. They kept on worshipping the Lord until they were totally consumed by the flames of divine love; they themselves became the offering."

So, this is one way, one easy way for us to meditate; it is to cry to God or to a God-realized person. It doesn't take any special effort to always be thinking of that person, that form, and when we're able to, when we're alone, to cry to them like Mirabai was crying to Krishna. Slowly, we'll become full of that Being, and then the vasanas will have no place to exist.

Amma gives the example of a body of salt water. How to get rid of the salt in the water? If we go on pouring fresh water into it, more and more, it gets diluted until it's virtually not there anymore. So, even though the vasanas are there, we may not be able to just root them out. What we can do is put something else in there so there's no space for them anymore. That's the thought of God, or our mantra, or Amma. This is the practical, easy way, for ordinary people like us.

The grace of a mahatma also is a saving factor. Amma has something to say about that also:

"Somebody said, 'I've read that no matter how much sadhana one does, the state of perfection can't be reached without the grace of a Realized Guru. Is this true?'"

Amma said, "Perfectly correct! In order to remove the subtler vasanas, one needs the Guru's guidance and grace."

It means not just the rough or gross habits that we have, but also the subtler things that we're not even aware of.

"And only the Guru can make those things manifest, bring situations that will make those things come out, and then give us the strength to deal with it. And when the vasanas are removed, the last stage, the point when a sadhak falls or glides into the state of Perfection cannot happen without the Guru's grace.

"Human beings are limited; they cannot do much on their own. Maybe they are able to proceed to a certain stage without anybody's guidance or help, but soon the way becomes complicated and help is required. The road to Liberation is a maze of intricate paths, a labyrinth. In traveling through the maze, a spiritual aspirant may not be able to figure out where to go, or which way to turn. Or following a spiritual path without a Guru can be compared to sailing alone in the ocean in a tiny boat that is not equipped with the necessary equipment, not even a compass to indicate the direction."

That's how hopeless it is if one is trying to realize God without the help of a God-Realized Master.

"Remember that the path which leads to the state of Self-realization is very narrow. Two people cannot walk together hand in hand, rubbing each other's shoulders in companionship along this path. One walks this path alone.

"As we walk on the spiritual path, there is a light that guides us. That light showing us the path is the Guru's grace. The Guru walks in front shedding light on the path as he slowly and carefully leads us. He knows all the intricate paths by heart. The light of his grace helps us to see and remove the obstacles and reach the ultimate goal."

We must exert ourselves; that's very important, but ultimately what saves us is the Guru's grace.

"The Sadguru's grace is what is needed the most. Without his loving care, compassionate glances and affectionate touch, one cannot reach the goal. With each compassionate glance and touch, he is sending forth his grace. Therefore, children, pray for his grace!"

Christmas
and the Mystic Christ -1

BEFORE AMMA CAME TO AMERICA, I HAD A DOUBT: how would people react when they saw her in Devi Bhava? Such a thing had never even remotely been seen here. But today I saw something very interesting that clarified a lot for me. I had totally forgotten about it. I saw a gentleman sitting in a store dressed up in a strange red outfit. People came up and sat on his lap. He gave a hug to each one of them and asked them what their wishes were. So it's no wonder that Western people could take to Amma like a fish to water. Of course, there's still a big difference between Amma and Santa!

Today is Christmas Eve, as everybody knows. And, for a spiritual person, the purpose of all these festivals is to increase his or her spirituality. Of course, Christmas has become a time to get together, to be with the family. It's also a time for commercialism— a time to profit for the businesses. But for us, for devotees, and perhaps the original purpose of Christmas also, it was to think about the personality of Christ, who was a great mahatma, and to read his teachings and his life.

Why is God So Fond of Dharma?

No country has a monopoly on sages, mahatmas and avatars. Whenever it's necessary, God, the Supreme Being, comes to this earth to bless living beings. In fact, in the Bhagavad Gita, there's a very famous verse in which Lord Krishna says that, when there's a need He comes. Now, what does God consider as a need? Probably all those people that come up to Santa Claus feel that they have a great need that they would like him to fulfill. People that come up to Amma also feel that whatever they need is a real need, very urgent, and that God Herself should fulfill it. But what does God feel is a need? Bhagavan Krishna says that when dharma is in decline and *adharma* is increasing, then, as far as He's concerned, there's a great need for Him to personally come to this plane of existence.

This is the verse:

> "Whenever there is a decay of dharma and an ascendency of irreligion, then I manifest Myself. For the protection of the good, for the destruction of evil doers, for the firm establishment of dharma, I am born in every age."
>
> —Ch. 4, v. 7-8

How is He born? Is He born like us? We're helplessly born into this world according to the fruits of our past actions, our karma. Bhagavan, God, is not born like that. He Himself says,

> "Though I'm unborn, of imperishable nature, and though I'm the Lord of all beings, yet ruling over My own Nature, I am born by My own Maya."
>
> —Ch. 4, v. 6

Of His own accord, He comes to the world out of compassion for the individual souls and to upraise or uplift dharma.

Why is God so fond of dharma? It must be a very important thing. Even His messengers cannot do that job. He Himself has to come and uplift dharma. So what is the great thing about dharma? Well, creation itself is a very mysterious thing. Nobody can say why it is here. The scriptures just say there was one Being alone before creation, *Brahman*. For those of you who don't know, Brahman comes from the Sanskrit word *brihat* which means great, or vast. That vast Infinity—the Universal Consciousness—that alone existed. Then It thought, "Let Me become many," and the universe came into existence. So this whole universe and all of us are just waves on the ocean of Brahman. The waves aren't different from the ocean, and they don't exist as separate from it. They may have an individual appearance—all of us seem to be individuals—but in the depths we're all one with that Ocean of Intelligence.

So after creation comes into being, what's next? What's the purpose? Bhagavan says that the world is like a school. Each lifetime is like a class. And the purpose is to graduate and get our post-graduate degree, which is called *mukti*, Liberation, *moksha*, Self-realization, the vision of God. That's the purpose of existence. That's the thing that's driving us on and on, the search for happiness, for bliss, and we can never reach that state of perfect satisfaction until we merge into the Source, our own Source. That's God or the Self.

All the lessons, all the experiences we go through in life are for that purpose, to take us back to the Source. And sometimes the lessons have to be very painful because we have many illusions. We're under illusion all the time—the cosmic illusion, Maya. We have to become disillusioned so that we're going in the right direction in a one-pointed way. This is the purpose of difficult situations, to disillusion us so that we wake up from the dream of Maya.

Bhagavan is concerned about His creation. We don't know why it came into existence, but it's here. And the one that created it is concerned about it, like a mother is concerned for her family or children. The scriptures, the sages, the avatars, have come into existence to show us the way to attain the goal of happiness. This is the importance of dharma, because that is the way back toe Him. It's not enough for us to just sit and meditate, or to do bhajans or listen to satsang. Spiritual life has to be practiced at every moment of our life, every thought, every word, every action. Then, when we're in tune with dharma, our mind will be in tune with God and we'll achieve the goal of life. We'll become happy. The more we become in tune with dharma, the more our mind will become peaceful and we'll become filled with bliss, the presence of God. So we have to study, "What is dharma?" We learn that from the scriptures, from sages, saints and especially from the lives of avatars and God-realized Souls.

Amma says a very nice thing about what causes God to come down. Somebody was asking the other day, "Christ was a God-realized person; he was an avatar. When he was nailed on the cross, it must have been extremely painful, wasn't it?"

Have you ever been pricked by a pin or a thorn? Just a little hole and you're in so much pain. Then what must have been his condition to have spikes nailed through his wrists and his feet? In that condition he said, "Oh Father, why have you forsaken me?"

After leading a whole life of devotion, surrender, and faith, how did those words come out of his mouth at that moment?

The Human Side of God

Amma gives the answer:

> "Children, once realization is attained, some beings merge with eternity. Very few of them come down. Who would like to come down after having entered the Ocean of Bliss? In order to come down from that state from which there is no return, it is necessary to have something to hold onto, a determined thought, a *sankalpa*. Only a few who can make that sankalpa to descend will come down.

> "That mental resolve is compassion, love or selfless service to suffering humanity. If you do not want to listen and respond to the call of those sincere seekers and the

cry of those who are suffering in the world, and if you want to remain in the impersonal state and do not want to be compassionate, it is all right. You can remain there.

"When you come down, a curtain, which you can pull away at any time, is put up by self-will in order to make functioning in this world smoother and uninterrupted. Intentionally you do not pay any attention to the other side of the curtain"

Which side? The side of oneness with God. Amma is speaking, of course, from her own experience. She never read any books. She never met any saints. From her own inner experience, she's talking.

"Yet on and off you do go to the other side, but you manage to come back. The very thought or reminder of the other side can simply lift you there. Once you come down then you play the role well."

This is the answer to the question about Christ: you play the role well.

"Once you've come down from oneness with God, you play the role well. You live and work hard for the uplift of all humanity. You'll have problems, obstacles, and difficult situations. You'll also have to face abuses, scandals, calumny, but you do not care because, although externally you look like everybody else, internally you are different, totally different. Inside you are one with the Supreme Truth. Therefore, you're untouched, unaffected. Having become one with the very source of energy itself, you work tirelessly, healing and soothing the deep wounds of those who come to you. You give peace and happiness to everyone. Your way of living life, your renunciation, love, compassion and selflessness gives inspiration to others to want to experience what you experience. If they do not want to be concerned about the world at all, those compassionate and loving ones who come down can also remain in that non-dual state and merge in Supreme Consciousness. In that state, there is neither love nor lack of love; neither compassion nor lack of compassion.

"In order to express compassion and love, and perform selfless service in order to inspire others to experience those divine qualities, one must have a body. Once a body is taken, it has to take its natural course. The mahatma's body is different from an ordinary person's. If he so wills, he can keep the body as long as he wishes without being afflicted by disease and suffering. But he consciously makes the body undergo all experiences that an ordinary human being undergoes. Therein lies his greatness!"

Seeing the life of Christ, or the life of Amma, some people express this doubt: "If they were divine, if Amma is divine, why does she have to go through so much suffering even now?"

When Christ was on the cross, the Pharisees and Sadducees came and said, "If you're the Son of God, come down from the cross!" It has nothing to do with being God-realized! God-realization means to be identified with God within, that there's a place within that's unaffected by anything else, even intense pain and suffering. And that place is always calm; it never changes. That's the core of their being. But, as Amma says,

"A God-realized soul gives the body to the world, and it goes its natural course. But it can be made to do exceptional things. Didn't Krishna get hurt during the Mahabharata War? Didn't He fight eighteen times with Jarasandha, the powerful and cruel king? Finally, He diplomatically left the battlefield. He could have killed

73

Jarasandha if He wanted to, but He didn't. Remember, it was an arrow shot by an ordinary hunter that put an end to Krishna's life in this world. Jesus was executed on the cross. Both of them could have prevented the events that put an end to their body, but they let everything happen in the natural course of events. They let life carry them. They chose to be as they were, and let the events occur.

"They were willing to surrender. However, this does not mean that the natural course is inevitable or unavoidable for them, as it is for ordinary humans. No, that's not so. If they had wished, they could have avoided all bitter experiences. Being all-powerful, they could have effortlessly destroyed those who opposed them, but they wanted to set an example. They wanted to show the world that it is possible to live with the highest values of life even while undergoing all the problems that an ordinary human has. Yet bear in mind that, if a circumstance arises where it is necessary for them to break a law of nature, they can."

So this is what Amma has to say about the nature of a Realized Soul, that they come down through compassion. They live like ordinary humans in most ways. If necessary, they can go beyond the laws of nature, as Christ many times did. And his saying, "Oh Father, why have you forsaken me?" was for those of us who, in great pain or suffering, also feel that way—that God has forsaken us. It's not so bad to feel that way when we're having so much anguish. Even Christ himself said it. So, he really showed his humanity, his humanness at that time; it wasn't due to weakness. It was out of compassion that those words came out of him. Because, shortly after that, what did he say?

"Forgive them, for they know not what they do."

So it's not that he forgot himself in that moment. Whatever comes out of a Divine Person is all for the good of humanity.

Since the purpose of an avatar is to give their teachings to the world, to inspire devotion to their personality as a means of getting devotion, I thought we would read some of Christ's words. I was surprised to find last year that there are many people that have never read anything of the New Testament. In fact, I also had never read the New Testament until I went to India.

Words of Christ

Every word, every single word, is a gem. Every word is a spiritual teaching, a gem of gems, and the diamonds of the teachings were words that he gave his disciples. There is the general public, and then there are the devotees, and then there are the disciples. The disciples will get the undiluted, distilled truth, and there are many portions in the Bible where he's speaking to the disciples.

> One day, as the crowds were gathering, Christ went up the hillside with his disciples and sat down and taught them there:

> "Humble men are very fortunate, for the Kingdom of Heaven is given to them."

Now, we should clarify some of our terms here. First of all, the Kingdom of Heaven may be another plane of existence in the vast creation—a place that is peaceful and blissful. But Christ said, "The Kingdom of Heaven is within you." So, it must also be a state of consciousness. When the mind becomes completely calm, then the inner Reality, which is hidden by the curtain of thoughts, starts to shine and one feels one is in Heaven. It means one is happy and peaceful. That's Heaven.

Also, many times he refers to the Father, like saying, "My Father sent me," and "I and the Father are one." When he says Father, what he's talking about is the Supreme Consciousness, the Absolute Being, Satchitananda, the Ocean of Awareness, the Source of Life, the Source of ourselves, the Source of all our awareness, the Source of the world. That's called the Father. Not that the Father is an old man with a beard, or maybe without a beard. But the Father is the Reality, the impersonal Reality. At the same time, that Truth can also be conceived of as God, the Father and Mother.

When Amma was a little girl, she used to go to a convent school for some years. At that time, sometimes she would sit in the church graveyard amongst the tombstones. She has said that many of the souls that had passed out of their bodies used to come to her and she would comfort them. She also used to go and see the image of Christ in the chapel. She would stand there and say, "You didn't die. I know that you didn't die!"

She told us that when Christ says the "Father," he's talking about Lord Shiva. Amma felt that Christ was a devotee of Shiva in the same way as she is a devotee of Devi. Apparently, even though a person may be a Divine Being, when they come into this world, they also have an object of devotion, either for the sake of others, or it's just inborn in them. Amma's God was Krishna and Devi and she felt that Shiva was the Lord of Christ. There are other examples also. Sri Ramakrishna's God was Kali, and Sri Ramana Maharshi's God was Arunachala.

There are many theories that Christ came to India during "the unknown years." The Bible is silent about his life after his twelfth year until his thirtieth year. It doesn't say anything about where he was until he suddenly reappears when he's thirty years old. There are many books saying that he went to India, he went to Tibet, he went to Egypt, and he went to so many places. We really can't prove anything conclusively, but, for me, Amma is my authority. She speaks from her own experience and says that when he says, "Father," he means Shiva.

"Those who mourn are fortunate, for they shall be comforted. The meek and the lowly are fortunate, for the whole world belongs to them. Happy are those who long to be just and good for they shall be completely satisfied. Happy are the kind and merciful for they shall be shown mercy. Happy are those whose hearts are pure for they shall see God."

This is the most important word in the whole Bible: if our mind is pure, we'll see God. If we are not seeing God, we have yet to fully purify our mind. What is meant by purity? Absence of thoughts is purity. The more thoughts, the greater the lack of purity. The ultimate purpose of meditation and other spiritual practices is to reduce the flow of thoughts so that the Real will shine forth.

"Happy are those who strive for peace, for they shall be called the sons of God. Happy are those who are persecuted because they're good, for the Kingdom of Heaven is theirs. When you are reviled and persecuted and lied about because you are my followers, wonderful! Be happy about it! Be very glad, for a tremendous reward awaits you. And remember, the ancient prophets were persecuted too."

Unfortunately, the world doesn't understand the Spirit, but the Spirit understands the world. This is the essence of what Christ is saying here. All these qualities are not qualities the people of the world want. The people of the world don't want to feel sad. They don't want to be meek. They don't want to be forgiving, full of mercy. It's an aggressive world. It's a competitive world. If we don't get out there and get what we want, we'll be left behind. That's the principle of the world. That's the principle of spiritual ignorance, Maya. That's not the principle of spirituality, that's not the principle of God-realized people and mahatmas. Christ is talking about the need for developing spiritual principles.

They are hard to practice, especially living in the world. That's the importance of *satsang* and reading the scriptures, so that we get exposed to the right ideas, because the world won't give us those ideas.

"You are the world's seasoning, to make it tolerable."

That means the saints and the sages make the world a good place. Otherwise it's not such a good place.

"If you lose your flavor, what will happen to the world? Then you yourselves will be thrown out and trampled underfoot. You are the world's light, a city on a hill glowing in the night for all to see. Don't hide your light; let it shine for all. Let your good deeds glow for all to see so that they praise your Father.

"Don't misunderstand why I have come. It isn't to cancel the laws of Moses and the warnings of the Prophets. No, I came to fulfill them and to make them all come true. With all the earnestness I have, I say, every law in the book will continue until its purpose is achieved. And so, if anyone breaks the least commandment and teaches others to, he shall be the least in the Kingdom of Heaven. But those who teach God's laws and obey them shall be great in the Kingdom of Heaven."

So, what is he saying here? That spiritual people are really "the salt of the world," they are the essence of the world. They are the ones that make the world a happy place. When we come to Amma, we feel such happiness, a unique happiness that we don't get through any materialistic means. That is the meaning. In the presence of a spiritual person there's a unique bliss—a happiness we can't get from the world. And such people, as she says, shouldn't hide themselves. They should be compassionate and mix with the world.

"Under the laws of Moses, the rule was, 'If you murder, you must die. But I have added to that rule and tell you that if you are only angry, even in your own home, you're in danger of judgment. If you call your friend an idiot, you are in danger of being brought before the court. And, if you curse him, you're in danger of the fire."

Now he's going one step further. Even small actions are important. The things we do with our mind are also important.

"If you are standing before the altar in the temple offering a sacrifice to God and suddenly remember that a friend has something against you, leave your sacrifice there, and go and apologize and be reconciled to him and then come and offer your sacrifice to God.

"Come to terms quickly with your enemy before it is too late and he drags you into court.

"The law of Moses says, 'If a man gouges out another's eye, he must pay with his eye. If a tooth gets knocked out, knock out the tooth of the one who did it.' But I say, 'Don't resist violence. If you're slapped on one cheek, turn the other too. If you're ordered to court, and your shirt is taken from you, give your coat too. If the military demand that you carry their gear for a mile, carry it for two. Give to those who ask, and don't turn away from those who want to borrow.

"There is a saying, 'Love your friends and hate your enemies.' But I say, 'Love your enemies. Pray for those who persecute you.' In that way, you'll be acting as true sons of God, for He gives His sunlight to both the evil and the good and sends rain on the just and the unjust too. If you love only those who love you, what good is that? Even scoundrels do that much! If you are friendly only to your friends, how are you different from anyone else? But, you are to be perfect, even as your Father in Heaven is perfect."

That's the goal, that we have to become one with God. Nothing less than that. We have to become perfect. It's quite unimaginable for most of us in our present condition to be perfect. "Be perfect" doesn't mean that we don't make little mistakes when we don't understand things. Perfect means that our conduct and thoughts are always in line with *dharma*; that our mind is always in a perfectly pure condition. It's clear like the sky. If we want to think, we can think, but we're not at the mercy of the mind. We can turn it off, or we can use it as we like. In such a mind, everything will be perfect. Perfect knowledge will shine in that mind.

Christmas and the Mystic Christ - 2

"Take care! Don't do your good deeds publicly to be admired, for then you will lose the reward. When you give a gift to a beggar, don't shout about it, blowing trumpets in the temple and in the streets to call attention to your charity. I tell you in all earnestness, they have received all the reward they will ever get who do so. But, when you do a kindness to somebody, do it secretly. Don't let your left hand know what your right hand is doing. And your Father, who knows all secrets, will reward you."

EVERY ONE OF THESE WORDS IS A SPIRITUAL TEACHING. In fact, Christ doesn't say anything except purely spiritual words. Some of Christ's teachings are about faith. Some are about devotion. Some are about renunciation. Some are about love. Here are some of his words about renunciation.

St. Francis of Assisi Meets the Pope

Many of us might have read about the life of St. Francis of Assisi. He was a true follower of Christ's ideal of renunciation. He felt that, if he was going to be a disciple of Christ, he should live just the way Christ had told in the scriptures, sowed in his life, and spoken in his words.

We could be disciples of Christ even today; in fact, that's the whole idea: to become a disciple of a God-realized person, not just to be a devotee. So, what did he do? He left everything and completely surrendered to the will of God. He led such a simple life! Just the barest necessities; simple food, the simplest dress. Simple means it was simpler than simple: he used to wear something like a gunny bag with a piece of rope tied around his waist like a belt!

Today, I had to go out somewhere and pass near a place where people were doing their Christmas shopping. I felt very strange because, for me, Christmas means thinking about Christ and his life of renunciation. His disciples were not caring about tomorrow or even today, about what they'll eat, where they'll sleep, or what they'll wear. And here are all these people running about shopping for things that couldn't possibly be necessities. It was such a strange feeling to see that.

Amma has a program every year in Assisi, which is where Francis was living. His holy presence is still felt there even though he lived there hundreds of years ago. Amma says that he was the real thing. That's a very rare comment for Amma to make. She doesn't say that often. People ask her questions about saints and sages and she'll smile or won't say anything. To say such a positive thing is unusual for Amma, unless the person is really an unusual person.

Francis and some of his friends and followers had renovated a dilapidated church with their own hands, and the local bishop and the local people became jealous. They came when he was away and burned the church down, and in the process, one of Francis' brother disciples was killed. Francis thought that he had done a very bad thing. Perhaps this whole undertaking, his renunciation of material life and rebuilding the old church, was a mistake because one of his brothers had died. So he decided to go to see the Pope in Rome. He thought the Pope was the representative of God. He must know everything. He'll certainly be able to tell him whether he's done the right thing or the wrong thing. So he went there.

He and some of his brother monks walked all the way. It is 175 kilometers from Assisi to Rome. That's a long distance to walk barefoot, in a robe or crude tunic, begging their food. They were not like us, who will get in a car, go sixty miles an hour, and stop at a restaurant on the way. That's our way of pilgrimage. No! In the cold or the heat, in the rain, barefooted, sometimes without food, for ten days and nights—that was their pilgrimage.

After reaching the Vatican, these beggars of God somehow got an audience with the Pope. They were true disciples of Christ.

I went to the Vatican when I was a teenager. It's overwhelming! The grandeur! The beauty! The vastness! The opulence! That's the thing that made the biggest impression on Francis—the opulence. He couldn't get over it. He couldn't believe it, because it had nothing to do with Christ. He looked this side and that side at the choir music and the hundreds of people, and the Pope sitting on a throne at the very pinnacle of this edifice.

All the courtiers were looking at them and holding their noses, thinking, "What are these dirty beggars doing here? How did they get in?" The Pope also was watching with a sceptical eye.

What happened next? Francis started quoting from the Bible, from the words of Christ. Here are some of the words he read out loud:

> "Don't store up treasures here on earth where they can erode away or may be stolen. Store them in heaven where they will never lose their value and are safe from thieves. If your profits are in heaven, your heart will be there too!"

Hearing this, those words pierced the heart of the Pope and he came down from his throne. When others heard Francis talking like this, they all rushed at him and started shouting, "What an insult! Why is he talking like this? Why is he talking like this?"

These were Christ's words that he was talking! It's not as if it were somebody else's words, or he made it up, or he was abusive. The founder of this vast church—Christ's own words! Well, they didn't understand. They took him and arrested him.

All the priests were pushing him out the door and then the Pope said, "Stop! Bring him back!"

They brought him back, and the Pope came over and said, "I was like you when I was young. I was full of earnestness to see God, to live the life that Christ told his disciples to live. But somehow or other, I got caught up in all this politics! I'm glad to see your innocence."

What did he do next? This is an eighty-year-old Pope and a twenty-year-old beggar boy. The Pope got down on his knees, put his head on Francis' feet and wept.

And other people in the church were thinking, 'Oh God, what's going to happen?'

"Don't worry!" one clever man said. "The Pope knows what he's doing. If he shows this kind of respect to this poor man, he will get all the poor people to again come to the Church."

Of course, that wasn't the Pope's intention. He wasn't that crooked; he must have been somewhat innocent to feel the way he did. He got up and went back and reluctantly sat on his throne. St. Francis left and went back to his little church in Assisi.

Christ said,

"If your eye is pure, there will be sunshine in your soul.
But, if your eye is clouded with evil thoughts and desires,
you are in deep spiritual darkness. And oh, how deep
that darkness can be!"

This means that, whatever the condition our mind is in, that's how we will see things through our eyes. If our mind is full of God, we see everything as God. A thief sees everything as something to steal. A good person sees everything as a chance to do some good. So everything we see is according to our mental outlook. The eyes are just windows through which everything goes into the mind, and there it's interpreted, something like sun glasses colour the vision. If we have green sun glasses, everything is green. So, if we have good qualities in our mind, everything is good.

Yudhisthira was the eldest son of the Pandavas, the famous Pandavas who were relatives of Sri Krishna. There is a saying that there was never an enemy born to Yudhisthira; he had no enemies. But Yudhisthira had so many enemies! In fact, half of the millions of people killed in the Mahabharata war were Yudhisthira's enemies! They were all out to get him. So, why is it said that he had no enemies? Because, as far as he was concerned, nobody was his enemy. He saw everybody as his friend. Because his mind was so pure, he never thought of anybody as an enemy, so he had no enemies! He was innocent. This is called purity of mind, or "a pure eye." Such a person always has the protection of God.

The Man Who Didn't Fear Mosquitoes

This is Christ's teaching about renunciation:

> "You cannot serve two masters: God and money; for you will hate one and love the other, or else, the other way around. So my counsel is, don't worry about things: food, drink and clothes. For you already have life and a body, and they are far more important than what to eat and what to wear. Look at the birds. They don't worry about what to eat. They don't need to sow, or reap, or store up food, for your Father feeds them. And you are far more valuable to Him than they are.

> "Will all your worries add a single moment to your life? And why worry about your clothes? Look at the lilies

85

of the field; they don't worry about theirs. Yet King Solomon in all his glory was not clothed as beautifully as they are. And, if God cares so wonderfully for flowers that are here today and gone tomorrow, won't he more surely care for you? O men of little faith!

So don't worry at all about having enough food and clothing.

"Why be like the heathen, for they take pride in all these things and are deeply concerned about them. But your Father already knows perfectly well that you need them and He will give them to you, if you give Him first place in your life and live as He wants you to."

These are not just words. These words are the experience of every sincere renunciate. It's very difficult to renounce all and to trust in God, but everyone who has done it has experienced the protection of God.

I once knew a person who gave up everything. He had nothing but two pieces of cloth, two *dhotis*, but they were very long so he could wrap them around the upper half as well as the lower half of his body. He took a vow that he was not going to ask anybody for anything, and would spend his life walking from one holy place to another. India is full of holy places, full of temples that have been founded by sages and saints over the ages. He decided he was going to spend twenty-five years like this, walking from one holy place to another.

In each holy place he would do sadhana, meditation, and watch the pujas. And he suffered a lot. He walked—never took a vehicle in twenty-five years! He went up into the Himalayas where it's really cold. Can you imagine going outside in the winter wearing just a T-shirt and shorts. So what about sleeping like that outside? For how long? Not just for a few hours—for twenty-five years!

One night, I was in the same room as him and there were so many mosquitoes there. I've never seen that many mosquitoes. Each one was about as big as a cashew nut! And there must have been at least fifteen or twenty thousand mosquitoes in a medium size room. It was like Vedic chanting was going on. You might have heard when many brahmins get together and chant the Vedas. How loud was it? The chanting of the mosquitoes was like that. But unlike Vedic chanting, it was unbearable! Someone gave me a mosquito net, which I covered myself with and I was somewhat peaceful except for the two or three mosquitoes that got inside and were driving me crazy.

And what was he doing? He was lying on a plank: no net, no blanket, no pillow, nothing. I had a mattress, a pillow, a blanket, everything. All he had was the other cloth that he wears. He just covered himself with it—a thin cotton cloth. And he peacefully slept away! He must have been eaten alive! But he didn't care. And then about two o'clock in the morning, he got up. He was sitting in the midst of all the mosquitoes chanting: "Ram! Ram! Ram! Ram!" till six or seven o'clock in the morning.

When I looked closely at him in the morning, I thought he'd be covered with blood. There was not even a mosquito bite on him. He had so surrendered to the will of God that God was looking after him. He never starved to death. He was alive after twenty-five years. He was skinny, but skinny doesn't mean weak. He was very strong.

When he would listen to bhajans, he would become ecstatic. He couldn't control himself and would get up. He would start to dance, run, shout, scream, and laugh. He would fall on the ground, laughing, because he had renounced the thought of everything except God. So when he heard bhajans, that's where his mind would go. He would merge into God and God is bliss.

God isn't some somber Being—God is the essence of bliss—so he would get immersed in bliss, in ecstasy.

Christ and the Rich Man

This doesn't mean that we all have to wander around in dhotis for twenty-five years in America up in the mountains, or anything like that. But we need to minimize, to not have unnecessary things. How many extra pairs of shoes and clothes and other things does each person have? It's unbelievable! Just what is necessary—have that. And all the rest, give it away. We don't need it. Even money. How much do we need? Keep what we need; the rest—give it away! This is what Christ was telling when the rich man came to him. What were those words?

> "Someone came to Jesus with this question: 'Good
> Master, what must I do to have eternal life?'"

Maybe he shouldn't have asked! Don't ask a God-realized person something unless you're ready for the answer. Really. Seriously, it's better you don't ask if you're not going to follow the advice.

> "What do I have to do for eternal life?"

He thought it was going to be something very simple: meditate five minutes twice a day and eat vegetarian food—something like that. What does Christ say?

> "When you call me good, you're calling me God. For
> God alone is truly good. But to answer your question,
> you can get to Heaven if you keep the commandments."
>
> "Which ones?" the man asked.
>
> "Don't kill. Don't commit adultery. Don't steal. Don't
> lie. Honour your father and mother, and love your
> neighbour as yourself."
>
> "I've always obeyed every one of them," the youth
> replied. "What else must I do?"

So, he already did all of that, and he still doesn't have eternal life. What is he doing wrong?

Here it goes:

"If you want to be perfect, go and sell everything you have, and give the money to the poor and you'll have treasure in Heaven. And come and follow me."

But when the young man heard this, he went away sadly, for he was very rich. Then Jesus said to his disciples, "It is easier for a camel to go through the eye of a needle than for a rich person to enter the Kingdom of God!"

It's not that somebody is standing up there at the Pearly Gates saying, "Are you rich? You can't get in. We let only poor people in here. It's just the opposite of earth." No. It means that, if the mind is occupied with earthly things, how can you think of God?

Or, if we take it from the point of view of the path of knowledge, if our mind is always outwardly bent, how can we make it abide in the Self? How can we have that quiet mind that reflects the light of the Self? Ninety-nine percent of the people who are wealthy are wealthy because they want to be wealthy. So their minds are occupied with that. Then how can they be thinking of God at the same time? Of course, there will be a rare group, one percent maybe, who have a lot of money because it was their fate, but who have no attachment to it. They don't calculate. They just spend according to the need and are very generous. And they could get up and leave it all in one minute, and never think about it for another second, never turn back and look the other way. So he's saying it's almost impossible for those attached to wealth to get into the Kingdom of Heaven. In other words, it's impossible for them to really meditate deeply.

This remark confounded the disciples—even the disciples! Not that they were rich. They just thought, 'What is he saying?

Does he mean that anybody who is attached to money cannot cannot reach God?'

> "Then who in the world can be saved?" they asked. Jesus looked at them intently and said, "Humanly speaking, no one. But with God, everything is possible."

So, by God's grace, even somebody who's very attached to wealth can realize Him. Nothing is impossible. In fact, by our own efforts, we're not going to realize God. But we do have to make efforts as much as possible, and the rest is left in God's hands.

Christ's Most Important Words

After Christ talked to the disciples and had done various miracles to instill faith into the people, he engaged himself in destroying the evil-doers. This was one of his objectives, to purify the society. He was not doing anything to them except destroying the evil in them so that the child in them, the divine child, the innocent child in them, could shine forth—just like Amma does. In those days, the Pharisees and Sadducees—the priests—were supposed to be the people who were to show the public the way to God. But they didn't care either about that or anything else truly religious. They were caring more about business. This is what Christ said to them:

> "You've turned this temple into a market place!"

He went in there and started knocking things down left and right.

> He said, "This is a den of thieves...!"

Everything was run by the priests in those days. Because they didn't have any truth in them, these priests couldn't accept his words. Later, they plotted against him and brought him to court. He was tried, convicted and executed. He was crucified.

It seems that, long before this, there were many godly prophets in Israel that had said at various points of time that things like this would happen. They said that somebody would be coming, an avatar. They called him the Messiah or anointed one. He would be the culmination of the dharmic life of all the people before his birth. It was all foretold what would happen—even the words that he would speak. And when they asked him, "Are you this one?" He said, "I am that one."

Even then, they couldn't accept it. So he was ultimately crucified. Before he died, he said:

"Father, forgive them for they know not what they do."

Amma says that this has to be our attitude; that we must get those qualities. Those mahatmas had the power to rectify the situation. They had the power to protect themselves, but they didn't. On the other hand, they stressed on forgiveness, mercy, and compassion.

Christ's words were the best thing that he could have said. It's the thing that we have to remember. Forgiveness and faith give us the strength to remain peaceful whatever may come

Three days after Jesus was killed, he resuscitated his body; he brought it back to life—child's play for such a person. He came to his disciples and talked with them. And just before he left this world for good, he said:

"Be sure of this, that I am with you always even to the end of the world."

Detachment - 1

THE OMKARA DIVYA PORULE SONG OF AMMA'S is concerned with the Vedanta or Advaita philosophy that says that we are the Atma, we are not the body. The body dies but not us, and that the bliss that we seek all the time, every day, every moment of our life, is not outside of us but it is our real Self.

Amma has not directly written any of these verses, but they are rather a collection of what she has said—her teachings. One of the brahmacharis wrote them down in the form of a song. Here is one verse:

> Tyagam manassil varanyal kurum tapam varum maya-mulam
> A satiraikiloklesam varum sarva nasam varum buvil arkum

It means, if the mind is devoid of renunciation, great suffering will befall one through illusion. If desire is not uprooted, affliction follows, which will culminate in the utter ruin of anyone in this world.

These are tough words. Obviously, Amma wants us to wake up to the Truth as soon as possible. But for most of us, we may need to go through the School of Hard Knocks before that happens.

Story of Bhartrihari

Bhartrihari was a great devotee and a king who later became a monk. He lived in the fifth century AD. One day, a sage came to him and gave him a fruit, saying, "If you eat this fruit, you will live a very long time." The king gave the fruit to the queen who was his favourite. The queen gave it to her boyfriend. Her boyfriend gave it to his girlfriend. His girlfriend gave it to her boyfriend. Like that, it made the rounds and finally ended up somewhere out in the city with somebody. That person felt that they weren't fit for such a thing and that the king was the fittest person for this wonderful fruit, so they came and gave it to the king. The king traced it back and found out that his wife was not faithful to him.

The realization that the one he thought was the dearest one to him, his wife, wasn't even faithful to him, that her so-called love was a sham—that woke him up from the sleep of Maya. He started thinking about more serious matters. He decided to leave the world in which he had spent his whole life seeking dreams. He became a sannyasi and went to live in a cave Ujjain, Madhya Pradesh. He did tapas for the rest of his life and wrote a hundred Sanskrit verses on renunciation. They are called the *Vairagya Satakam* and are in Sanskrit and they are superb. There's probably no book written on detachment or renunciation like this. Another similar work, called *Bhajagovindam* by Sankaracharya, is also concerned with the same topic of the transitory nature of the world, the illusory nature of worldly happiness, and the greatness of Self-realization.

Vairagya Satakam is like a commentary on Amma's teachings. Why does she stress so much on renunciation? As we've said so many times, renunciation does not mean becoming a sannyasi and going off into the woods or living in an ashram and doing tapas. Everybody has to practice a certain amount of renunciation, even in daily life.

Suppose we come home from school. Tomorrow we have an exam, a test, but our mind says, "I want to watch the TV." Our intellect says, "No, no, I've got to do my homework or I'm going to flunk the test." What are we going to do? Are we going to follow what our mind and senses say or are we going to follow what our intellect says? Are we going to go for the computer games or are we going to do our studying? Hopefully, we put the temporary pleasure aside and go for the long-term benefit. That's called renunciation.

Actually, we are all doing that much of the time. If we want to succeed in anything, we have to exercise a certain amount of control over our mind and senses, because the very nature of the mind and senses is to wander. It's natural to feel that happiness is outside in sense objects; that's everybody's experience, but if we just let our senses run wild and do whatever they want, that will just destroy us. We will have no concentration. We won't be able to do anything properly. We'll end up in a pit.

The *Upanishads* give the example of a person driving a chariot and holding onto the horse's reins. If we just let go of the reins and let the horse run, what's going to happen? It's going to go off into a pit by the side of the road. Then we are going to get hurt. So we have to learn how to hold the reins and control the horses. Our senses are just like that. If we don't learn that, then we have to suffer. It doesn't matter who we are. That's Nature.

Suppose there's a flame burning on a gas stove. And suppose we don't know what fire is. We are very young—only one year old. Seeing the pretty flame, we start to think, 'It's so nice! It's so pretty!' And then we stick our little finger into it. What's going to happen? It's going to get burnt. We can't tell the fire, "I'm just a little girl. I didn't know you were going to burn me. You shouldn't have burned me." We can say that, but fire is not going to care about us. The laws of nature are such that they don't care who goes against them. They don't care how innocent we are, or how ignorant we are. Those are the laws. So the senses, they don't care anything about us, they have their own nature, the mind has its own nature. But we, the soul, the *Atman*, have to learn how to control them if we want to have a peaceful existence and not a scattered life.

Amma says that self-control can be taken to the maximum, that the mind can become so controlled and so calm that it merges into its source, that we can attain the state of Self-knowledge. If we want to experience who we are, that we are really the immortal Atman and not the body, the mind has to become completely calm for that experience to arise. From the viewpoint of bhakti or devotion, that is also the criteria for realizing God. The extroverted tendency of the mind has to be curbed, both for worldly improvement and spiritual realization.

Parikshit and the Srimad Bhagavatam

Many of us might have read the Srimad Bhagavatam. It contains stories of Sri Krishna's life and the lives of the incarnations of Lord Vishnu. It also contains the lives of many of Lord Vishnu's devotees and of many kings. It's a recounting of ancient Indian history and is also full of many spiritual lessons.

It's being told to a king named Parikshit, who had only seven days to live. It was his fate that he was going to be bitten by a very poisonous snake and die. When he heard that news, he perceived life in a very different way than before. Until then, he had been enjoying life. When he heard that he was going to die in one week, everything changed. He realized, 'What was the use of everything that I did in my life? What's the use of my kingdom, my family, my wealth, my prestige, my health? It's all going to go down the drain in one week. Isn't there something more lasting than this?'

Because he was a spiritual person, he knew that the Self, the Atman, the vision of God was more worthwhile than the passing things of the world. So he sat down by the side of the Ganges River and started to meditate.

Why meditate? Because the mind is so restless that we have to somehow calm it down to get some inner peace. One of the processes to attain this is meditation. When we reach the stage when we want to experience peace, then we feel that the world of the senses is a great distraction. We start to feel the stress that the senses are putting on us. All five of them are running in different directions. They always want to be stimulated and satisfied. Some people—having experienced everything they wanted through their senses and still not getting satisfaction—realize, "What a terrible thing this is! My senses are pulling me apart! Even though I don't want it, they are persisting." That pulling outwards is due to *vasanas*.

Amma gives an example of what is meant by vasana. We make a decision, "I'm not going to do that anymore," but the past habit makes us do it again. She gives the example of the dog and the jackal. Whenever the jackal would go by, the dog would start barking. Then the dog decided, "I'm not going to waste my time like this. Why should I bark at the jackal?" But the next time the jackal went by, sure enough, the dog started barking again.

Or the cat who wanted to learn how to read and write. There was a cat that got fed up with catching mice. It thought, 'There must be a better way to make a living than always running after mice. Suppose I learn how to read and write. I could probably get some employment, temporary of course.' So the cat got a book through a correspondence course. It use to sit up at night with a candle and would read the lessons. Everything was going along okay for about a week. Then, one night, a mouse ran by. The cat just knocked over the candle and went running after the mouse, forgetting all its lessons.

That's vasana. We make a decision: 'I'm not going to do this thing anymore—whatever it may be.' Then, when the situation comes in front of us, again we do it! This is another reason for trying to cultivate self-control and renunciation, so that we don't have to dance to the tune of our senses and our habits.

The king was trying to meditate, but he couldn't. When we are very thirsty for the state of inner peace, for whatever reason—either because we suffered a lot or we had a glimpse of some spiritual state or we met a mahatma like Amma—whatever the reason is, when we really get thirsty for that, then our teacher comes. We don't even have to go looking for a master or a guru. It will happen. That meeting has to happen. That's the spiritual law of nature.

When Parikshit was sitting there struggling, the great mahatma Suka arrived. Not only him, but also so many mahatmas came with him. He was going to initiate Parikshit in a very unique way—by telling him a long story. It took him seven days to tell the story. That was the Srimad Bhagavatam. At the very end, Suka said, "I told this whole thing about the nature of the universe and what spiritual life is all about and devotion and meditation and wisdom and detachment only for one reason—just so that you would get a feeling of dispassion towards sense objects. Because only if that dawns on you, will you be able to experience the peace and bliss of your own soul."

Because of his devotion to the Lord and the imminence of death, the words of Suka revealed the true nature of the world to Parikshit. He closed his eyes after seven days of hearing Bhagavatam and tore the veil of illusion; his mind came to a perfect standstill; it stopped. In that still mind, he saw his real Self. He lost all body-consciousness, all world consciousness. If we have no body-consciousness, we have no world consciousness also. Just as in sleep, when we lose our body consciousness, there's also no world for us. He lost all external consciousness, but he was fully conscious of his real Self within. While he was in that state, the snake came and bit him and his body died, but he didn't even know it, for he was forever merged in the bliss of the Atman.

Desire and Renunciation

Renunciation—in the sense of being able to turn off the mind, to turn off the senses and to keep perfectly still, trying to get the inner vision—is very necessary. We get this through satsang, through a person like Amma's presence, or through the stories in the scriptures. Vairagya Satakam was written for that purpose. Of course, Bhartrihari must have been written it primarily as an outpouring of his own experiences, but it was also written for the good of others.

> "All glory to Shiva, the Light of Knowledge, residing in the temple of the yogi's heart, who smites away like the rising sun, the massive front of the endless night of ignorance, overcasting the human mind, in whose wake follows all auspiciousness and prosperity, who burnt up Cupid as a moth as if in sport, and who appears beaming with the rays of the crescent moon adorning His forehead."

Bhartrihari's ishta devata, his deity, was Lord Shiva, so he starts his work with a prayer to Shiva. He's praising Shiva. I'm not going to read every single verse. There are a hundred verses, and I'm only going to read about thirty of them.

> "Worldly pleasures have not been enjoyed by us, but we ourselves have been devoured."

I'm sure all of us have, at some time or another, eaten too much. The food was so delicious. We enjoyed it, but we couldn't stop eating. So what happened? What started out as a pleasure ended up as a pain, as a tummy ache. That's what the senses do.

Moderation is okay, but if we don't control the accelerator, so to say, then instead of us eating them, they'll eat us.

"No religious austerities have been gone through, but we ourselves have become scorched. Time is not gone, but it is we who are gone because of the approach of death. Desire is not reduced in force, even though we ourselves are reduced to senility."

Amma says that however old a person is—even a hundred-years-old—desire will always be like that of a sixteen-year-old. Just because we see an old person, don't think that they don't have any desires. Their desires are just as strong as those of a sixteen-year-old youth.

"The face has been attacked with wrinkles. The head has been painted white with gray hair. The limbs are enfeebled, but desire alone is rejuvenating."

The body is falling apart, but desire is not getting any weaker; that's its nature. Unless we do something about it, it's not going to get weaker with age. Don't think like this: 'When I'm eighty years old, I'm going to stop all worldly activities and go to an ashram and meditate.' Desire is not going to stop by itself and it is desire that makes the mind and senses restless. It's that force which makes our mind run outwards.

"Though my friends, dear to me as life, have all taken such a speedy flight to heaven, though the impulse for enjoyment is wearied out, and the respect commanded from all persons lost, though my sight is obstructed by cataracts and the body can raise itself but slowly on a staff, still—alas for its stillness—this body startles at the thought of dissolution by death."

Even though my body is falling apart and I'm so old I can hardly get up with a stick, still, when I think of death, I tremble.

"Hope is like a flowing river, of which the ceaseless desires constitute the waters. It rages with the waves of longing, the attachments for various objects are its animals of prey. Scheming thoughts are the birds, and it destroys in its course the big trees of patience and fortitude. It is rendered impassable by whirlpools of ignorance and of profound depth. As it is, its banks of anxious deliberation are precipitous indeed. Such a river the great yogis of pure mind pass across to enjoy supreme bliss."

The idea that we are going to be permanently happy through something or other outside of ourselves is due to the cosmic illusion called Maya.

Our whole spiritual life is only trying to go beyond the force of Maya. If we want to travel to space, or we want to go beyond the pull of gravity, what do we have to do? If we just sit here, it's not going to happen. We need a rocket. Then, when it reaches a certain speed, it can escape from gravity.

We could sit here on earth forever. Gravity is not going to let go; that's its nature. The same is the case with Maya; it's never going to let us go. It's not that it's cruel or that it's wicked or that it's a bad joke. That's just its nature. Fire is not cruel. It has a purpose. Can we imagine if there was no gravity? What would be going on? We would all be floating around in the room, and if we go outside, we would float out to space. Gravity is necessary.

If we want to escape from the force of Maya, if we don't want to dance to the tune of what our senses always tell us, if we want to be free of the illusion that happiness is possible through any temporary thing, we have to fight. We have to fight as long as necessary until we have escaped. That's called moksha or Liberation or Self-realization. How much do we have to fight? How frequently do we have to fight? It's like saying, "How frequently do I have to fly to get beyond gravity?" We have to fly until we're beyond it.

This is the importance of constant effort in spiritual life, constantly reminding ourselves of these truths. This is why, even though we are coming here every week, I am saying the same things again and again. If nothing else, it's refreshing my memory. Every time I hear myself talk about the higher truths of spirituality, it gives me a shake that will hopefully wake me up, even though it may only be temporarily.

The body is ultimately going to die. Even though it is getting older, desires are not getting less. Considering the amount of effort that we have put in towards being happy, it always seems to last only for a short time.

> "The objects of enjoyment, even after staying with us for a long time, are sure to leave us some time. Then what difference does their privation in this way make to men, that they do not of their own accord discard them?"

The law of karma says that, whatever we give away will come back to us when we need it. Bhartrihari is saying that, even though we know that we can't hold on to the objects of our enjoyment—that either they are going to leave us or we are going to leave them— why is it that we can't give them away before that? If enjoyments leave us of their own initiative, if they tear themselves away from us, they produce great affliction of mind. Suppose somebody steals something from us, or suppose there's a disaster in our business—something's lost, everything's lost—we feel miserable, but it wouldn't be the same if we had given that thing away. Then we'd feel happy.

If people voluntarily renounce objects of desire, that will conduce to the eternal bliss of Self-realization. We don't want to give in order to get; that's not the idea; that's not the principle we are trying to learn here. That's business. But if we give, then we gradually won't want to get anymore and we will be happy. It's the wanting to get, the desire, that makes us miserable, makes us mean, makes us restless. When we don't want to get anymore and we want only to give, then what we get is something quite different than what we give. We get peace. Nothing else can give that except renunciation.

> "Blessed are those who live in mountain caves meditating on Brahman, the Supreme Light, while birds devoid of fear perch on their laps and drink the teardrops of bliss that they shed in meditation, while our life is fast ebbing away in the excitement of revelry in palatial mansions or on the banks of refreshing pools or in pleasure gardens, all created and brooded over merely by imagination."

Blessed are those who live in the bliss of meditation on God and who shed tears of *ananda*. Birds sit on the laps of such people because they have no fear of them. The worldly are, on the other hand, absorbed in pleasure. The last part of this verse is very important but easy to miss. Bhartrihari says that all those pleasures are actually created by and thought about through imagination. If there was some intrinsic happiness in pleasurable objects, they should always be pleasurable. However, we find that such is not the case. Depending on the attitude of the mind, something that is pleasurable at one time might be painful at another.

> "For food I have what begging brings, and that too, tasteless, and once a day. For a bed, the earth. For an attendant, my body itself. For dress, I have a worn-out blanket made up of a hundred patches and still, alas! desires do not leave me."

Even though I possess almost nothing and have renounced everything, I am still unable to renounce desire. Such a strong thing it is!

"Without knowing its burning power, the insect jumps into the glowing fire."

Have you ever seen that—an insect flying into a fire or a hot light bulb? It is very sad that it has no knowledge of what is going to happen to it. And how are we humans any different? Even though we can reflect before doing anything, we also feel attracted by so many things that may end up giving us trouble or even death.

"The fish, through ignorance, eats the bait attached to the hook, whereas we, having full discernment, do not renounce the sensual desires, complicated as they are with manifold dangers. Alas, how inscrutable is the power of delusion!"

Neither Amma nor the scriptures say that everybody should become a yogi and live in a cave, or that nobody should pursue worldly life and have a good time. She is saying that one should have the knowledge of the true nature of worldly pleasure and pain, and not get lost in that.

We need to keep this knowledge in our 'back pocket', because if, at some time in our life, we find that our search for happiness through sense pleasure and worldly life doesn't work out, then we'll have something to fall back on; we'll remember these words on detachment. Then we can make an attitude adjustment and lead a more spiritual life aimed at divine bliss and peace.

"When the mouth is parched with thirst, man takes cold refreshments. When suffering from hunger, he swallows cooked rice made delicious. When set on fire by lust, he embraces his partner. So happiness is but the remedy of these diseases, of hunger, thirst, and lust. And behold, how man is upset in its quest!"

He's comparing the thirst of the senses to a kind of disease. This is one way to think of it. Our senses get restless, they get stimulated, they get agitated, and then to get rid of that irritation, we do various things. This is what our life is like—lighting a fire and then putting it out.

"Possessed of tall mansions, of sons esteemed by the learned, of untold wealth, of a beloved wife, and thinking this world to be permanent, men deluded by ignorance, run into this prison-house of the world, whereas blessed indeed is he who, considering the transience of the same world, renounces it. The pit of our stomach is so hard to fill, and it is the root of no small undoing."

Why does he say that? Because, if we didn't have to eat every day, we'd have a lot less problems. Apart from the pain of hunger, indigestion and overweight, we wouldn't have to make so much money if we led a simple life, because we wouldn't need special food. We have to eat because we have to live. If we were able to live under a tree with a minimal amount of clothing, that would be enough.

"It is ingenious in severing the vital knots as it were of our fond self-respect."

Many people will throw away their self-respect in order to be able to satisfy their stomach.

"It is like the bright moonlight shining on the lotus that blooms only in the sun. It is the hatchet that hews down the luxuriant creepers of our great modesty."

"And in enjoyment, there is the fear of disease."

If we are sick, we can't enjoy properly. Suppose we like to eat but have a weak stomach, or we don't have teeth? Suppose we like to see nice things, but our eyes don't work properly. Suppose we like to hear sweet music, but we are hard of hearing. So, if we have any kind of disease, enjoyment is a problem. It could also mean that the loss of energy that is used during enjoyment may result in illness.

"In social position, there's the fear of falling off if your happiness depends on social position. In wealth, there's the fear of thieves; in honor, the fear of humiliation; in power, the fear of foes; in beauty, the fear of old age; in the body, the fear of death.

All the things of this world pertaining to man are attended with fear. Renunciation alone stands for fearlessness. Health of men is destroyed by hundreds of ailments of the body and mind. Wherever there is Lakshmi, there, perils find an open access."

What's meant by this? Lakshmi is the goddess of wealth and prosperity. Wherever there is prosperity, there is also an open door to misery because prosperity has so many complications. Most people in this world don't think in this way. 'If there's prosperity, there's happiness; all our worries will be over,' is the normal way of thinking, but a spiritual person won't care a fig for prosperity. Their wealth is the wealth of inner peace. They may use their prosperity without attachment for the good of the world.

Goddess Lakshmi and Swami Vidyaranya

Swami Vidyaranya was the Prime Minister of king of the Vijayanagara kingdom during the fourteenth century. He eventually became a sannyasi and the head of the Sringeri Sankara Peetam. This Prime Minister had a desire to be prosperous and wealthy, just like everybody else does, so he did all the pujas to Lakshmi. He did them three times a day. He did ten thousand mantra repetitions. He used to do Lakshmi's mantra. Day and night, he went to the Lakshmi temples. He did so many vows in order to get Lakshmi's grace so that he would become wealthy.

He went on like this for years but he didn't become wealthy. He got fed up and realized, 'Why am I giving so much energy for this? My life is ebbing away.' He decided to become a sannyasi and try to realize God, to attain Self-realization. So he left the house. He put on his sannyasi clothes, the ochre cloth, but, just then, a dazzlingly beautiful woman appeared before him. It was none other than the Goddess Lakshmi!

He said, "Can I do something for You, Devi?"

"You have been praying to Me all these years. Now I have finally come."

"Now You have come and now I don't want You."

"I have to give you something."

"Okay, give me the wealth of spiritual knowledge. Give me the wealth of Realization." So she blessed him that he would be a wise man full of scriptural knowledge and spiritual experience. He got the name Vidyaranya because of the blessings of Lakshmi. "Vidyaranya" means one who is a forest of learning.

So, seeking Lakshmi for wealth will end up at a dead-end ultimately, because of all the problems that we've been discussing here—death, enemies, thieves, and all the things of which the world is made.

"Whatever is born, dies."

Is there anything created by the Creator that is stable? No.

"Enjoyments of embodied beings are fleeting, like lightning in the clouds. Life is as insecure as a drop of water on a lotus leaf. The desires of youth are unsteady. Realizing this, quickly let the wise firmly fix their minds in yoga, easily attainable by patience and equanimity. Old age looms ahead, frightening men like a tiger. Diseases afflict the body like enemies. Life is flowing away like water running out of a leaky vessel. Still, how wonderful that man goes on doing wicked deeds!"

Detachment - 2

ALL OF US ARE ASLEEP, DEEP ASLEEP IN THE DREAM world called Maya or universal illusion, and the only way to wake up is through intense spiritual practice and detachment from the dream.

This isn't the only teaching of Amma's. Amma also teaches that through intense devotion to God, through surrender to God, through various devotional paths or through the path of selfless service, the mind can wake up to its true nature, the immortal Self.

We are talking about Vedanta and the need for *vairagya* or detachment. I'll explain what I mean by vairagya in a moment.

When we say that we are asleep in Maya, "Maya" means that force which makes us forget Reality, which is always there and makes us take what's in front of us as real and then gets us into trouble. Not only do we forget Reality, we forget even realities.

Suppose there's a very little boy, one and half or two years old. Before he knows anything about this world, we put some gold coins in front of the little boy and also put some cookies in front of him. Which one do you think the little boy is going to take? Cookies, of course. Why? The little boy doesn't know that with the gold coins, he could buy mountains of cookies. He sees only the immediate pleasure that is right there in front of him. He is not thinking about long-term investments or anything like that.

This is what Maya is: we see the immediate pleasure, the immediate happiness that a thing gives us, so we go for it and ignore everything else, like the long-term consequences.

How to wake up from Maya? Amma says that vairagya is the essential thing. Even Sankaracharya—you might have heard of him—also says that we may have no other good quality except that, and that would be enough for us to attain Self-realization, to go beyond the cycle of birth and death. So what is this vairagya? Vairagya means lack of, or the absence of *raga*.

Raga is not only a type of tune in Indian music. It also means attraction or attachment to a thing. Our mind is always going between either attraction towards things or repulsion from them, and sometimes indifference. So, lack of attraction or lack of attachment is vairagya. This is the thing that will wake us up from the dream. It's because of our attachment and attraction towards the dream of Maya that we stay asleep.

That attraction generates energy and brings about birth after birth. It becomes very complicated because, as long as we're asleep, the law of karma holds true. Everything that we do in this dream has its action and reaction. The only way we can break this wheel or break this cycle is to wake up. That means we have to withdraw our mind from the dream, and then it will break. When we break the dream, that awakened state is called *bodha* or Enlightenment, Self-realization, or Liberation from the cycle of birth and death or Release.

Samartha Ramdas and Shivaji Maharaja

Samartha Ramdas, who lived in Maharashtra during the seventeenth century was a great devotee of Hanuman and Lord Rama. He emulated all the qualities that Hanuman had: devotion to Sri Rama, service and renunciation.

When he was twelve, his widowed mother wanted to get him married. During the marriage ceremony, the boy and girl sat facing each other with a cloth or a curtain between them. Just before they were about to meet and get married, the priest would say, "*Savadhan* (be alert!)" Ramdas was spiritually inclined from childhood, so, when he heard "Savadhan," it flashed in his mind,

'I'd better beware! Am I sure I want to get into this complicated situation? Have I understood all the implications? Is everything going to be all right? What will happen to my spiritual life?' So that one word brought up all these thoughts. Immediately, and to everyone's surprise, he jumped off his seat like a monkey, and ran out of the marriage hall as fast as he could. After that, nobody saw him for the next twelve years. This is called intense detachment.

Vairagya may start out as fear of the suffering and other complications of worldly life, but he was destined to become a monk, and that is why it happened like that. One word was enough. Nobody had to explain anything to him. Also, he wasn't calculating, 'If I do like this, what's going to happen? If I don't that, what's going to happen? Should I do this or should I do that?" No, his vairagya came from a deep conviction that worldly life would be an obstruction to his spiritual progress. Very few people feel like this, but those who are destined for sannyasa develop this kind of vairagya at some point in their life. They don't procrastinate. They feel that there is no other way of life for them.

So, he jumped, he ran to a forest and started doing intense spiritual practices. He would stand in a river up to his neck in cold water in the winter time doing his *mantra japa*. He spent all his waking hours in various forms of worship, tapas and study. He repeated his mantra 130 million times! All this sadhana was aimed at developing more detachment from his physical existence and the world, and to merge in the Self, the soul. He finally attained perfection by Sri Rama's grace.

One day, when Ramdas went begging, he happened to pass by the royal palace of his disciple, Shivaji Maharaj. He had his begging bowl—a coconut shell that was hollowed out. He would go to each house and say, *"Biksham dehi cha Parvati,"* "Oh, Divine Mother, please give me alms." When he came to the gates of the palace, Shivaji came running out. The Guru held out a bowl to the disciple. Ramdas said, "Please give me alms." Shivaji took out a pen and a paper, wrote down something, and put the paper in the bowl. Ramdas said, "What is this? Is this paper going to satisfy my hunger?"

"Please, read the paper, Swamiji."

What was on the paper? Shivaji had signed over the kingdom to Ramdas! "The kingdom is yours. I don't want any more to do with it. This is my alms to my Guru. I only want to serve you."

This is not unbelievable. There are people who do that even today. They have so much love for and faith in their Guru, and are fed up with the world. Without calculating, they give everything to their Guru. A true devotee must be fearless, like someone ready to jump off a cliff, not knowing what's going to happen; and, just before hitting the ground, something catches him and softly places him on the ground.

So, Shivaji gave the whole kingdom to Ramdas. He read the note and said, "Thank you very much, but you keep it in trust for me. You look after it for me." This is real vairagya, for both of them! The disciple had real detachment; the Guru had real detachment. Nobody wanted the kingdom!

This is a practical example of what is vairagya. This is what is needed to make the mind steady. It is lack of vairagya, lack of detachment that makes our mind so restless. It's always running after one thing or another. If it gets one thing, it stops running for a few moments. Then again, a new desire rises up in the mind. It wants to run after something else. It never stands still more than a second or two except when we go to sleep or when we are in *samadhi*. Most of us have never been in samadhi, so it's mostly when we're in deep, dreamless sleep.

Eventually, we get fed up with this constant restlessness. At that stage, we are starting on our way back to the real Self. We're on our way back to God. We have to reach that stage where we can say, "I've had enough of this endless restlessness. Whatever I've gotten, whatever I've done, I still didn't get peace. There is no real peace in anything of this world."

There's a beautiful verse written by a mahatma describing this nature of how we have to eventually go back to the Self or God; it is inevitable. Every being will have to reach that stage, the stage of real vairagya. Here's the verse:

"The waters rise up from the sea as clouds, then fall as rain and run back to the sea in streams; nothing can keep them from returning to their source. Likewise the soul rising up from Thee cannot be kept from joining Thee again, although it turns in many eddies on its way. A bird that rises from the earth and soars into the sky can find no place of rest in midair, but must return again to earth. So indeed must all retrace their path, and when the soul finds the way back to its source, it will sink and be merged in Thee, O Arunachala, Thou Ocean of Bliss!"

—Sri Ramana Maharshi

This is what is happening to us. We are like the water that's risen up from the sea, fallen back to the earth, and becomes a river that flows this way and that until it reaches the sea. Or like a bird that rises up into the sky but ultimately has to come back to the earth.

What is the source from which we have arisen and into which we will return? The Ocean of Bliss, God or Self.

Fear of Death

King Parikshit heard that he was going to die in a week, and so he gave up everything and sat and meditated and realized God within one week. Amma says that if we have that kind of intensity, even one moment is enough.

Parikshit was very detached, very intense to realize God, and also very afraid of death. There is nothing wrong with that. In a way, it's good to be afraid of death because that energy of fear will spur us on to do spiritual practice.

So what did he do? He did a very interesting thing. He heard that he was going to die by a snakebite on the seventh day hence, so he had a pillar constructed—a very tall pillar. It must have been fifty or a hundred feet tall. On the top of the pillar there was a room, and there was no way to get up and down the pillar, except by a rope. That's how he got up there. He was sitting in the room doing his meditation and whenever food was to be given to him, he used to lower down a basket and then he would pull it up with the fruits and other things. That's how he was eating for these seven days. He had stationed around the bottom of this pillar his entire army, so if any snake comes, they will flatten it like a chappati or a tortilla!

Well, what happened? The snake that was destined to bite him was no ordinary snake. He was a very smart snake. The snake turned himself into a little worm, not even an earthworm, a tiny worm, and bored his way inside one of the fruits that were going to be sent up for breakfast on the seventh day. When Parikshit lifted up the fruit and was about to bite into it, the worm poked out its little head, smiled at him, turned into a big snake and bit him. Finished. When it's our time to go, we'll go. We may be up in the sky or under the earth or in our bedroom or on the highway or on the moon. When our time's up, nothing can prevent it. As Lord Krishna says in the Bhagavad Gita,

> "Just as a man casts off worn-out clothes and puts on others which are new, so the embodied casts off worn-out bodies and enters others which are new. To that which is born, death is indeed certain, and to that

which is dead, birth is certain. Wherefore, about the unavoidable thing, thou ought not grieve."

—Ch. 2, v. 22, 27

Now we are going to read some of Bhartrihari's verses. Each one is a gem. When we are reading this, don't listen to it like poetry or philosophy. Try to take each one into your heart, because that's what they were written for. They are to wake us up, for just a moment at least to get a glimpse of the nature of Maya, because we are so deeply asleep in it. It's unbelievable how deeply asleep we are.

"Old age looms ahead frightening men like a tigress. Different diseases afflict the human body like enemies. Life is flowing away like water running out of a leaky vessel. Still how wonderful that man goes on doing wicked deeds!"

This is not to say that there is nothing good in life or we shouldn't enjoy life, but we should understand the painful side of life also. Spiritual life means to understand everything, not just to be enamoured and ignore the true nature of things. We can see the pleasant side of life, but we have to see the other side also, the painful side of life—both sides of the coin. That's real wisdom. Especially for us who are only used to looking at the pleasant side, this is very necessary so that we see things in a more balanced way.

"Manifold and transitory in nature are the enjoyments, and of such is this world made up. So what for would you wander about here, O man? Cease exerting your-selves for them, for if you put faith in our word, on its supreme foundation, the Reality, and concentrate your mind, purified by quelling hope with its hundred meshes, free yourself from desire."

Desire makes us run after transitory things. Even though we may not get what we want, hope that we will become happy thereby keeps us going after a will-o'-the-wisp, a goal that cannot be reached. Bhartrihari is saying to have faith in the words that he is telling us now. They are born out of his experience of Reality. Give up hope in our desires so that our mind will become calm.

> "There is one enjoyment, and one alone, lasting, immutable, and supreme of which the taste renders tasteless the greatest possessions, such as the sovereignty of the three worlds, and established in which the gods Brahma, Indra, or the others appear like particles of grass. Do not set your heart on any ephemeral enjoyment other than that."

Spiritual life doesn't mean giving up enjoyment. It means that we want an upgrade to a higher bliss. Somebody's got an ordinary Ford, next they want a Mercedes Benz, then a Rolls Royce. And when one is bored with a Rolls Royce, then what? Probably a Bentley.

We have a little house, and then we think it would be much better if we had a bigger house. Then we get the bigger house, and then that's not enough, so we think, 'I wish I had a still bigger one.' Then we see someone who has an even bigger one than that. How far can we go? There is no end to enjoyment, and there's no ultimate satisfaction. There can never be. So this is what he is saying: there is one enjoyment that will satisfy us forever and that will make even the position of being the highest gods in the universe look like grass.

That's what Amma also says. There's a song where Amma is describing her experience and she says,

> "I saw everything as my own Self, and the whole universe as a tiny bubble in my own vastness."

That's the experience we need. If we wake up from this sleep, then we will see the whole universe as a tiny bubble in our eternal vastness. That's the enjoyment of supreme bliss. That's the aim of spiritual life.

"Don't run after anything else but that. Don't waste your energy. Don't waste your time. Don't get into all these complications of Maya."

"Where in some home, there once were many, there is now one; and where there was one or many, there is none at the end."

Understand? In one home there were so many; then there was only one, and then after some time, even that one wasn't there anymore.

"This is the process in which expert Father Time plays his game on the checker board of this world with living beings as the pieces to be moved, and casting the two dice of day and night. Daily with the rising and setting of the sun, life shortens, and time is not felt on account of affairs heavily burdened with manifold activities. Neither is fear produced at beholding birth, death, old age, and suffering. Alas, the world has become mad by drinking the wine of Maya."

Life is slipping away every day, every night. It is getting shorter. We are so busy with so many things, we don't even notice it. We are drunk with the wine of Maya. Amma says that even if we don't have much suffering, we should go somewhere where there is suffering so that we can understand the nature of this wheel of time—how merciless the law of karma is. When we see people that are really suffering, we should think, 'That could happen to me also.'

"Seeing even the same night to be ever following the same day, in vain do creatures run on their worldly course, persevering and busy with various activities set a going secretly by their mental resolves. Alas, through infatuation, we do not feel ashamed at being thus befooled by the cycle of birth and death with occupations in which the same particulars repeat themselves again and again."

A cow always goes on chewing the same cud again and again. Our life is like that: we go on doing the same things again and again. We go on having the same experiences again and again, but still we go on. We don't think of trying to go any higher than our ordinary mundane life. This is Maya.

"Those from whom we were born, they are now on intimate footing with Eternity."

They are long dead.

"Those with whom we were brought up have also become objects of memory. Now that we have become old, we are approaching nearer to our fall day by day, our condition being comparable to that of trees on the sandy bank of a river."

If a riverbank is sandy, and there is a tree growing there, what will happen to the tree? It will die, and when it dies, what will happen? It will mix with the sand and decompose. In the same way, we are on the sandy bank of the river of time. There is no firm bank on the river of time. The river of time is wearing away the sand under the roots. Finally the tree is going to fall down and decompose.

"Now a child for a while, and then a youth of erotic ways, a destitute now for a while, and then in abundance, just like an actor makes at the end of his role, when diseased in all limbs by age and wrinkled all over the body, his exit behind the scene that veils the abode of death."

Now we are young, then we get older, then we get still older, and then we exit the scene. The world is a stage. Remember when you were a child? It was all gone too soon. Then all the responsibilities of being older, and then for some of us, old age has come. Then the next step is death. Then what comes after death? Rebirth.

"Being agitated, O mind, you now descend into the nether regions. Now you soar up into the skies. You wander all around the four quarters. Why, even by mistake, do you not once concentrate on the Supreme Reality of the nature of your own Self, bereft of all imperfections, whereby you may attain supreme bliss?!"

Our mind wanders everywhere except where it should go, which is to our own Self. It's like a river that comes out of the mountains. It goes everywhere. It never goes back to its own source, but that's where it has to go eventually. We learn so many things, we know so many things, we experience so many things, and finally we reach a point where we want to get back to the source. We're convinced that there is nothing anywhere except to rest in the Self. This is what happens when we go to sleep. However much we know, however much we experience, however much we have, at the end of the day, we don't want any of it. We just want to forget it all and go to sleep. Because when you go to sleep, what happens? We forget everything, because being busy with all these things is very tiring after some time. But, however much we sleep, we don't feel that we don't want to sleep anymore. We have to get up because we have to do other things, but sleep is such a happy state. That's a glimpse of the Self but veiled by the darkness of spiritual ignorance. But bliss and rest and peace are experienced then.

At the beginning of spiritual life, it's like that. The mind will think of everything except God, everything except the Self. This becomes even more so when we try to meditate. Amma says by pouring fresh water in a vessel of salt water, the salt water gradually becomes diluted to the point of nonexistence. Similarly, if we go on pouring the thought of God or our mantra into the distracted mind, that one thought will replace of the many. Finally, a stage will be reached wherein only God shines.

This takes a lot of practice, but it's not impossible. Those who have attained Self-realization did this. Most of them were not born mahatmas. They weren't born with concentration. Very few are born like that. They worked hard at it. The mind is a thing that can be moulded. It can be made to concentrate and become one-pointed. In that condition, it can experience Brahman or the Reality. That's what spirituality is all about—training the mind.

Amma gives the example of the coconut tree climber. Those of us who have been to Kerala know there are millions of coconut trees everywhere, forests of coconut trees. How do we get the coconuts off the coconut tree? We have to climb it. There is no other way. So, suppose we are born in a family of coconut tree climbers. That most probably means that we are going to become a coconut tree climber when we grow up. One day, our father is going to say, "Listen, I think it's about time that you learn how to climb up the tree." So we get on the tree, we try to climb up, we go up about a foot, and then come crashing down. Then we try it again and come slipping down. Then we try it again and feel discouraged. We say, "I can never get up this thirty-foot tall tree. I can't even go one foot! Forget it. I'll become something else; I'll become a farmer."

Then our father will say, "No, you have to become a coconut tree climber. There is no other way for us. That's been our occupation since thousands of years." So what do we do? We try again and again. Next time we get one foot two inches, and again we come sliding down. But the idea that we have to do it, that there is no other way, keeps us going. We keep getting higher and higher. Finally, we get right up there at the top of the tree. We are throwing down the coconuts. It took a lot of practice, a lot of persistence, but we succeeded!

In the same way, all of us have to try to climb the tree of the mind and reach the top which is up here on the top of the head— the thousand-petal lotus where God is sitting in Bliss—and then, when we get adept in going up, everything will be fine. Until then, we have to go on trying, thinking that there is no other way. It's like a journey. To where? Inside, not outside.

"In old age, the body becomes shrivelled. The gait becomes unsteady. The teeth fall out. The eyesight is lost. Deafness increases. The mouth slavers. Relatives do not value one's words. The wife doesn't care. Even the sons turn hostile. Oh, the misery of a man of worn-out age!"

We don't like to hear all this, but this is the truth. These are realities. It is not the Reality, but the facts of life.

"As long as this body is free from disease and decrepitude, as long as senility is far off, as long as the powers of the senses are unaffected, and life is not decaying, so long wise persons should put forth mighty exertion for the sake of their supreme good, for when the house is on fire, what is the use of digging a well for water?"

When the house is on fire, then what are we going to do? The first thing we would probably do is try to get water to put it out. If we have a tap or a faucet, we open the faucet and get the water. What if we don't have a tap or a faucet? We could try a river, but if we don't live near a river, and we don't have a tap or a faucet, then we must be having a well. If we don't have a well, then we would have to start digging a well. But there is no sense digging a well when the house is on fire. Likewise, there's no sense trying to do intense spiritual practice or trying to control the wandering mind when our body is already falling apart. Why? Because the mind is busy with the collapse. How can it concentrate? How can it apply itself to anything? So before that stage is reached, apply all our energy to realizing our Self.

> "When honour has faded, wealth has become ruined, those who sue for favours have departed in disappoint-ment, friends have dwindled away, retainers have left, and youth has gradually decayed, there remains only one thing proper for the wise: residence somewhere in a grove on the side of a valley of the Himalayas where the rocks are purified by the waters of the Ganges."

Bhartrihari is trying to inspire us with sublime thoughts. He's exposed the world for what it is, now what to do? Should we become sad? Should we become miserable about it? No. We should think, "What's the alternative to this situation, this condi-tion?" He's saying that when all these things have happened and we have understood the nature of the world, then think of living in an ashram or in a hut in the Himalayas on the banks of the Ganga and doing our spiritual practice there. Otherwise, at least we can go to a holy place and do sadhana.

Detachment - 3

DURING THE PAST TWO WEEKS, WE'VE BEEN TALKING about how we're so deep asleep in Maya that we don't even know that we are asleep. The purpose of such books like Vairagya Satakam is to shake us and wake us up so that we get a glimpse of the Truth. From there, we can start to lead a spiritual life, start to do sadhana.

Marriage of Narada Maharshi

There's a very interesting story about Maya, about how one forgets everything and one doesn't even *know* that one's in Maya and how one thing leads to the next and to the next and to the next and it gets deeper and deeper and finally, hopefully we cry out to God and we start to wake up.

You all might have heard of Narada Maharshi. Narada is one of the celestial sages. He's not an earthling like us. He lives in the subtle planes of existence. After we leave the physical body, which we all will, then we don't cease to exist; we live in a subtler plane of existence. There are many such worlds called *lokas*. Narada lives in those subtle worlds, but he can manifest on the earth. He has manifested many times. He's considered a very great mahatma, a very great sage.

One day, he was sitting in the Himalayas doing tapas. He was meditating, very deeply absorbed—not completely absorbed, but very deeply absorbed. Seeing him, the gods, especially Indra, the king of the gods, started to get a little worried because the gods are not enlightened beings and have some very human qualities ,like jealousy and fear.

To become a god, they did a lot of good actions in their previous life, like a lot of charity and Vedic worship and other pujas. They were not interested in Self-realization, but more to gain worldly ends and to live in the heavenly worlds. In the old days, that was how people used to achieve a very difficult thing, something which they thought would be impossible otherwise. They would resort to doing tapas, doing prayers and penance, various vows and so on. The gods reached that level of existence through their tapas. They are more powerful than humans, but they are not saints or sages.

Indra's got a peculiar quality: even though he's the king of the gods, he's always worried that somebody is after his position. So when he saw Narada sitting there doing tapas and japa and meditation, he thought, 'Narada's after my position. He wants to become the king of the gods.' Actually, Narada couldn't care less because he's full of God Himself. Indra usually puts an obstacle in the way of the *tapasvis*, people doing tapas, and it's usually the same obstacle. He sends down damsels, the dancing girls of heaven. They are called *apsaras*. He also has various other means. I'll tell you about one other means he has.

There was another occasion where there was a yogi who was doing tapas. As usual, Indra got upset and decided to spoil the yogi's tapas. This yogi had taken a vow to conquer his tongue—his sense of taste, so he would eat only dried leaves that had fallen from the trees.

Knowing this, Indra sent a messenger down with a basket full of *papadams* (a thin crisp, like potato chips). Everyone likes papadams, even yogis! Indra's man broke the papadams into pieces and mixed them with the leaves on the ground.

When the yogi finished his meditation, he went to pick up the leaves to eat a few, and noticed that they had a new taste. Leaves don't taste very good. They're kind of bitter, but these were exceptionally tasty leaves. Eating those "leaves," he started getting fatter and fatter. He was getting sleepy when he was doing his meditation because he was getting so stout. He was always thinking about the next time when he could go and eat those delicious leaves. This way, his tapas was destroyed by Indra.

Of course, this is may be just a story, but these things happen to us also. When we try to go higher in spiritual life, I don't know if it's Indra or who it is or what it is, but various obstacles come from somewhere to divert us.

So Narada was doing tapas. Indra decided to send down some apsaras, some damsels who were supposed to distract his mind from his deep concentration. They were dancing and singing with their *tablas* and *mridangams* and harmonium. But Narada didn't open his eyes. They tried their best, but nothing happened. He still didn't open his eyes, so they got discouraged. They went back and told Indra, "We failed."

After sometime, Narada opened his eyes; he was just in meditation, not samadhi. He thought, 'I must have really attained Perfection because I wasn't affected by those apsaras.' He felt a little proud, and so he went to Mount Kailas. He wanted to brag to somebody about how great he was. Reaching Lord Shiva's presence, he said, "Shivaji, did you hear? I was doing tapas and Indra sent so many damsels to distract me, but it didn't phase me at all. I wasn't distracted at all. I didn't even open my eyes though I knew what was going on."

Then Shiva said, "Oh, that *is* wonderful! You are really a great mahatma! You are perfect! Listen, one thing; it's okay that you told Me, but don't tell Vishnu," (because Vishnu is the Guru and the God of Narada). "Be sure you don't tell Vishnu about all this."

Well, naturally, when somebody says, "Don't do this," the first thing we start to think about is to go and do it. Amma has told a story about a sick person who went to a doctor to get some medicine. The doctor told him, "Whenever you take this medicine, don't think about a monkey or it won't work." So when the man went home and was taking the medicine, he immediately started thinking about a monkey. He couldn't take the medicine! So if you tell somebody not to do a thing, that's the thing they are always going to want to do.

Immediately, Narada went to Lord Vishnu and said, "Did You hear the news? I have become perfect. I am unaffected by the divine damsels."

Vishnu said, " Oh, that's wonderful! I'm very happy to hear that, Narada. I knew that you were great—now I know that you are perfect! Come on, let's go for a walk."

They went for a walk, and as they were walking, Vishnu led Narada into a desert. It was very hot. Vishnu said, "Narada, I'm so thirsty! Can you just bring me a glass of water from somewhere?"

"Oh, yes, Bhagavan. Just let me look around." He left the Lord, and as he was searching, he found a village about a mile away and entered it. There was a well and a beautiful girl pulling up water from it. Narada said, "I would like to get a glass of water for somebody."

The girl said, "No problem. Come to my house. I'll get the glass and give you the water."

So they went to the house. The more Narada looked at the girl and talked to her, the more he started to appreciate her. Finally, he decided to get married to her. Maya! In fact, it had started even before that when he became proud of himself.

He asked the father of the girl if they could get married.

The father said, "Sure."

They got married, and then Narada got involved in the business world. In the village, he started a business, had three or four kids, and about seven or eight years passed like this.

One day, there was a tremendous storm and the river near the village became flooded. Water started to spread everywhere. The river was rising and rising and entered into Narada's house also. Everybody—the wife and children, climbed up onto the roof, but still the water was rising. Everybody was getting worried. One by one, the kids were washed away, and then the wife was washed away. Narada was so miserable. When the river started to pull him away too, he screamed, "Vishnu, Narayana, save me!" at the top of his lungs.

Until then, he hadn't even thought about Vishnu or Narayana. As soon as he cried out, the water subsided, the village disappeared, and he was standing there right next to Vishnu.

Vishnu looked up at him and said, "Narada, where is my glass of water?" Eight years had gone by in all that complicated Maya. So this is what Maya is all about. We started out in God. Somehow we ended up in Maya. We become very involved in Maya and at some point, we cry out to God. Something happens in this dream of Maya. We find some loophole or there is something wrong, we don't want to continue in this dream any longer, and then we cry out to God. That's the beginning of the end of the dream. Then we go back where we came from, to God.

This is possible, and it usually happens due to the association with a mahatma. Otherwise, of our own accord, that doesn't happen. The blessings of a saint or the company of a saint like Amma or maybe a saint that we can't even see, who has left their body, could also bless us. Maybe we read a holy book that we might have read many times, but when we read it this time, it has such an impact; it completely changes our lives. We have become serious about spiritual life.

Lord Ganesh, the Merchant and Beggar

This reminds me of another story. I think it's a true story, although I can't testify to that because I didn't see it myself, but I heard about it. There were some tourists in India going to various tourist places. There was a forest on the outskirts of one of the towns where they were touring and they went into it. They thought there must be some nice place in there, maybe even a temple. After going very deep into the forest, they found a sannyasi sitting under a tree. One of them said, "Swamiji, we are tourists. Do you know of any nice place around here that we could visit?"

The Swamiji replied, "Actually, if you keep going another few miles, you will come to a village. There's a wonderful Ganesh temple there and that Ganesh is no mere Ganesh. It's not just a stone image. It's a living being."

"Oh, Swamiji, that's a bunch of nonsense. How can you say that?"

"No, I know it for sure. I'll tell you a story of what happened there. In that village, there were two people very devoted to Ganesh. One was a very wealthy merchant and one was a blind beggar. The blind beggar used to sit in front of the temple the whole day long with a little piece of cloth spread on the ground, expecting a few coins from the devotees. The wealthy merchant used to go there every morning and would go into the Ganesh temple and pray, 'O Ganesh, please give me a hundred thousand rupees today in my business—one lakh rupees.' In the evening, he would come back. Usually he was very successful, so he would again thank Ganesh.

"One day, the beggar devotee got nothing to eat. He got no money. Nothing! He also had a family. His family was starving. He went to the temple. He was in tears. He went up to Ganesh and said, 'Ganesh, how can You leave Your child like this, starving?

I and my family had nothing to eat yesterday. We got no money. Why are You so indifferent to us? Why are You so cruel?'

"Crying, he left the temple. Just at that time, the merchant was going into the temple when there was a sound inside. There were two voices that were talking, one female and one male voice. The lady said, 'Son, why are you so indifferent to your devotee? Why can't you shower some grace on him? He's been sitting here for so many years.' Then the male voice said, 'You are right, Mother. By tomorrow afternoon, I'll make him a millionaire.' Who was that? That was Ganesh's mother, Parvati Devi.

"The poor man didn't hear that, but the merchant heard everything. He put two and two together. He figured out what was going on. He was very clever. He was also very crooked. He did his *namaskar* to Ganesh, came out of the temple and went over to the poor man and said, 'I'll give you a hundred rupees, under one condition: that whatever you get tomorrow from your begging, you give it to me.'

"Well, the beggar knew that he's not going to get anything more than a few pennies, a few paisa, so he said, 'This is a great deal. Sure, you can have anything I get tomorrow. I'll take the hundred rupees.' He took the hundred rupees and went and bought food for his family. He was very happy.

"The merchant couldn't even sleep that night, he was so excited. He was going to get at least a million rupees the next day. Next day he came at eleven o'clock and sat around waiting. Nothing, not even a penny was put in the beggar's bowl. Then he waited till noon, but nothing had happened. It was one o'clock, and still nothing happened; two o'clock, nothing happened. He was very frustrated. He went into the temple and started to shout, 'What kind of God are You? I lost my hundred rupees believing in You!'

"Then suddenly he felt something catching him around the neck. He looked down. It was an elephant's trunk. It was squeezing him and pushing him against the wall. Then a voice said, 'You crooked fellow. Right now you'd better scream out to your accountant. Tell him to come here.' So he screamed until the accountant somehow heard about it and came running. The voice said, 'Now, tell him to give a million rupees to that poor beggar.'

"So he gave the million rupees to the beggar. And after that, because of the touch of Ganesh, this man's mind completely changed. That evening, he went home, gave half his wealth to his family, and distributed the other half to all the poor people that he knew. Then he went and sat under a tree and started doing spiritual practices. He surrendered to God and attained peace of mind."

The tourists who were hearing this story said, "Swamiji, it's a very nice story, but how could we believe that such a thing could happen, that a stone Ganesh could come alive and catch somebody around the neck and talk? Did you see that person? Can you give us any proof? Do you know anybody that saw this?"

With a peaceful look on his face born of his inner experience, the swami said, "I was that merchant."

Bhartrihari Continues

This is how somebody changed due to the touch of God. This is, of course, extremely rare and even difficult to believe, but there are many people who have changed due to the touch of Amma, and who have led a spiritual life from that time onwards. Once we've changed and decided to pursue the Eternal, once we've started to see the world as transitory, that our body, wealth, and family are passing away right before our eyes, that we are also decaying, and that the so-called deep affection and attachment that everybody seems to have for each other can so easily evaporate at any moment, then what do we do next? That's where we left off in the Vairagya Satakam last week. After exposing the nature of Maya, of worldly life, and giving us a shake, then Bhartrihari continues:

"When honour has faded, wealth has become ruined, those who sue for favours have departed in disappointment, friends have dwindled away, retainers have left, and youth has gradually decayed, there remains only one thing proper for the wise: residence somewhere in a grove on the side of a valley of the Himalayas where rocks are purified by the waters of the Ganga."

Once we have reached that stage when all the delusions or illusions of the world have left us, when we see that there is nothing worthwhile in the world, then what is the next thing to do? Go to the bank of the Ganga in the Himalayas to do sadhana to realize God; this is what Bhartrihari did. This was his experience and path.

"Delightful are the rays of the moon. Delightful the grassy plots on the outskirts of the forest. Delightful are the pleasure of wise men's society. Delightful are the narratives and poetical literature. Delightful the face of the beloved swimming in the teardrops of feigned anger. Everything is charming, but nothing is so when the mind is possessed by the evanescence of things."

All these things are so beautiful—the beautiful green grass on the hills, beautiful poetry, the society of good people, the rays of the moon, the face of the beloved. But once your mind has woken up to vairagya, once you see that everything is evanescent, it's passing away right in front of your eyes, nothing is so delightful anymore.

"Desires have worn out in our heart. Alas, youth has passed away from our body. Virtues have proven barren for want of appreciative admirers. The powerful

all-destroying unrelenting Death is fast hastening in.
What is to be done? Ah, me! I see no other refuge left
except the feet of the Destroyer of Cupid."

Who is the Destroyer of Cupid? Lord Shiva. The story goes that
the gods wanted Lord Shiva to have a child for their own purpose
of destroying a demon who was troubling them. So, Cupid was
sent to get the deed done. While Lord Shiva was sitting in meditation, Cupid shot a flower-arrow at Him to make Him wake
up and fall in love with the Goddess and make a child. His third
eye opened up, and the god of love, Kama, was burnt to ashes.
The meaning is, of course, that only if your third eye opens up,
only if the vision of the Self or God-realization dawns, can *kama*,
or the sex desire, be completely destroyed. Transcending the sex
urge however, is possible only in the state of God-realization.
So Bhartrihari is saying that there is no other refuge for him to
cross the Universal Illusion except the Lord.

> "Sitting in peaceful posture during nights when all
> sounds are stilled into silence, somewhere on the banks
> of the heavenly river Ganga which shines with the white
> glow of the bright diffused moonlight, and fearful of
> the miseries of birth and death, crying aloud, "Shiva!
> Shiva! Shiva!" Ah, when shall we attain that ecstasy that
> is characterized by copious tears of joy?"

When will be able to sit in the moonlight by the side of the Ganga
crying out to God, afraid of the miseries of birth and death? When
will we experience the bliss of God-realization, when the tears of
ecstasy roll down our cheeks?

> "Giving away all possessions with a heart filled with
> compassion, remembering the course of destiny which
> ends so ruefully in this world, and as the only refuge for
> us, meditating on the feet of Shiva, Oh! we shall spend

in the holy forest nights aglow with the beams of the full autumnal moon."

So, what is the rueful end of our destinies? Death.

"When shall I pass the days like a moment, residing on the banks of the Ganga in Varanasi, clad only in a strip of cloth and with folded hands raised to my forehead, crying out, "O, Gaurinatha, lord of Gauri, Tripurahara, slayer of Tripura, Shambo, giver of all good, Trinayana, the three-eyed, have mercy on me!"

When will that day come that I can live in Kashi on the banks of the Ganga crying out to the Lord?

"Those who have only their hand to eat from, who are contented with begged food, who repose themselves anywhere, who require no house or bed, who constantly regard the universe as a blade of grass, who, even before giving up the body, experience the uninterrupted Supreme Bliss, for which yogis, indeed, the path which is easy of access, by Shiva's grace becomes attainable."

Some sannyasis don't have even a begging bowl. They only go to a house and hold out their hand for alms.

'Oh Mother Lakshmi, Goddess of wealth, please serve someone else. Do not be longing for me. Those who desire enjoyment are subject to You, but what are You to us who are free from desires?

Everybody in this world—except for the sannyasis—is praying to Lakshmi because they desire wealth, prosperity, enjoyment, and pleasure. But sannyasis don't have material desires; they want something more than worldly happiness or worldly pleasure. They want the bliss of God-realization. So Lakshmi, please don't come to me. Go to those people who want You.

"The earth is his bed. The arms his pillow. The sky is his canopy. The breeze is his fan, the moon is his lamp. And rejoicing in the company of renunciation as his wife, the sage lies down happily and peacefully like a monarch of undiminished glory."

What a beautiful image this is! To a mahatma, Mother Nature is his all. The breeze is his fan, the moon is his lamp. Detachment or renunciation is his wife and he lies down like a king in great glory on the earth, his bed.

"Will those happy days come to me, when on the bank of the Ganga, sitting in lotus posture on a piece of stone in the Himalayas, I shall fall into samadhi, resulting from a regular practice of meditation on Brahman, and when even antelopes, having nothing to fear, will rub their limbs against my body?"

Will those days ever come when I will sit in samadhi in the Himalayas and be so absorbed in God that even antelopes will mistake me for a tree and rub against me?

This is the last verse:

"O earth, my mother, O wind, my father, O fire, my friend, O water, my relative, O sky, my brother. Here is my last salutation to you with clasped hands. Having cast away Maya with its wonderful power by means of an amplitude of pure knowledge resplendent with merits developed through my association with you all, I now merge into the Supreme Reality, Brahman."

With the blessings of the Universe, and transcending the Divine Power of Maya through Self-realization, I bow down to you all and merge into Eternity, the absolute Brahman.

Bhajan as Sadhana

"At dusk the atmosphere is full of impure vibrations. This is the time when day and night meet and this is the best time for sadhaks to meditate because good concentration can be obtained."

WHAT DOES AMMA MEAN WHEN SHE SAYS THAT the atmosphere becomes more impure at the time of dusk? Wherever there are humans, their negative adharmic thoughts and feelings like anger, jealousy, miserliness, revenge, selfishness and so on emanate from their minds and stay in the atmosphere. This is also the case with their good or dharmic thoughts. Unfortunately, most peoples' minds are full of thoughts motivated by selfishness. This may be one reason why the ancient sages used to live in forests rather than in villages and cities. Forests are considered as *sattvic*, villages as *rajasic*, and cities as *tamasic* (pure, active, dull).

Mother Nature has three aspects. One is *sattva*. Sattva means calm, serene, tranquil. Think of a body of water that is very calm or when we are standing on the top of a mountain and look over a vast expanse. How does our mind feel at that time? That's a sattvic feeling.

Then there is *rajas*. Rajas is activity, restlessness, ambition, heat. The colour of that is red. The colour of sattva is white.

And then *tamas*. Tamas is inertia, dullness, mistakes, error, sleep, laziness, indifference, stubbornness. The colour of tamas is black. It's inert.

In the Bhagavad Gita, Lord Krishna divides mankind into two categories: divine and demonic.

The Blessed Lord said:

1. Fearlessness, purity of heart, steadfastness in knowledge and Yoga; alms-giving, self-restraint and worship, study of one's own (scriptures) austerity, uprightness;

2. Harmlessness, truth, absence of anger, renunciation, serenity, absence of calumny, compassion to creatures, non-covetousness, gentleness, modesty, absence of fickleness;

3. Energy, forgiveness, fortitude, purity, absence of hatred, absence of pride; these belong to one born for a divine lot, O Bharata.

4. Ostentation, arrogance and self-conceit anger as also insolence, and ignorance, belong to one who is born, O Partha, for a demoniac lot.

5. The divine nature is deemed for liberation, the demoniac for bondage. Grieve not, O Pandava; thou art born for a divine lot.

6. There are two creations of beings in this world, the divine and the demoniac. The divine has been described at length; hear from Me, O Partha, of the demoniac.

7. Neither action nor inaction do the demoniac men know; neither purity nor good conduct nor truth is found in them.

8. They say, "the universe is unreal, without a basis, without a Lord, born of mutual union, brought about by lust; what else?"

9. Holding this view, these ruined souls of small intellect, of fierce deeds, rise as the enemies of the world for its destruction.

10. Filled with insatiable desires, full of hypocrisy, pride and arrogance, holding unwholesome views through delusion, they work with unholy resolve;

11. Beset with immense cares ending only with death, sensual enjoyment their highest aim, assured that is all.

12. Bound by hundreds of bands of hope, given over to lust and wrath, they strive to secure by unjust means hoards of wealth for sensual enjoyment.

13. 'This today has been gained by me; this desire I shall attain; this is mine, and this wealth also shall be mine in future.

14. 'That enemy has been slain by me, and others also shall I slay. I am a lord, I enjoy, I am successful, strong and healthy.

15. I am rich and well-born. Who else is equal to me? I will sacrifice, I will give, I will rejoice.' Thus deluded by ignorance,

16. Bewildered by many a fancy, entangled in the snare of delusion, addicted to the gratification of lust, they fall into a foul hell.

17. Self-honored, stubborn, filled with the pride and intoxication of wealth, they perform sacrifices in name with hypocrisy, without regard to ordinance.

18. Given over to egotism, power, haughtiness, lust, and anger, these malicious people hate Me in their own and others' bodies.

19. These cruel haters, worst of men, I hurl these evil-doers for ever in the worlds into the wombs of the demons only.

20. Entering into demoniac wombs, the deluded ones, in birth after birth, without ever reaching Me, O son of Kunti, pass into a condition still lower than that.

21. Triple is this, the gate to hell, destructive of the self: Lust, Wrath and Greed. Therefore, these three, one should abandon.

Ch.16, v. 1-21

This is a very exhaustive list of human traits. One of the reasons to hear this is for us to see what demonic qualities we still have and what divine qualities we don't have. The mind is not something that is cast in stone. It is dynamic, always changing according to our thoughts, words and deeds. We can strive for being in the divine category and renounce the demonic. In fact, we have to. Although Amma does not speak to us in such unequivocal and plain words, she also lays a lot of stress on purifying the mind of its negativities through sadhana and good conduct.

With all this subtle junk in the atmosphere, is it any wonder that, at the end of the day, it is so impure? All of these thoughts will effects us a lot. Mahatmas are very sensitive to the thoughts and vibrations in the atmosphere around them. They perceive the powerful effects of thoughts, good and bad. In the Bhagavatam, it is told that one of the reasons that sages travel to holy places is to purify those places by their divine presence. Since God shines in their hearts, they are the greatest purifiers of the earth. Amma also sometimes jokingly refers to herself as a vacuum cleaner of souls.

In spite of all its subtle pollution, dusk is the best time for spiritual practice. Perhaps this is because Nature is winding down, giving way to the night, and it's a time of relative quiet and peace. We must remember that we are part of Nature and can feel its different changes if we pay attention. Those who can clearly feel them tell us that this is the best time to meditate.

The evening and morning times, just after the sun sets and just before it rises, are considered very sensitive for the mind. Tradition has it that whatever one does during those times will leave a deep impression or vasana in the mind. For this reason, one is not to engage in worldly rajasic and tamasic activities like eating and sleeping. Doing so will increase the urge to do so again and again at those times. On the other hand, doing sattvic actions at those times will increase ones divine nature.

There is a story in the Bhagavata about this very principle. Diti, the mother of the *asuras* (anti-gods) wanted to make love with her husband, the sage Kashyapa. Since he was doing his daily worship and it was the evening time, he told her to wait a while and then he would satisfy her. Unfortunately, she could not control her passions and forced him into the act. Due to this, she later gave birth to two asura brothers, Hiranyakasha and Hiranyakashipu who were both killed by Lord Vishnu. The moral of the story is be clear enough: don't have sex during the evening time if you want sattvic children.

What Amma says here is:

"If sadhana is not done, more worldly thoughts will rise up. That is why bhajan (singing religious songs) should be sung loudly at dusk. In this way the atmosphere also will be purified."

During this time, our predominant nature becomes stronger. If we are mostly spiritual, we will become more spiritually minded at that time. Our tendency to meditate, pray or do bhajan, will increase. We will intuitively feel like doing these things. Worldly people, who don't have any spiritual tendencies, will feel more inclined towards worldly activity, pleasure, enjoyment, sleep and so on. Indulging at that time will strengthen such tendencies. Amma is saying that a sadhak should use it in the best way possible and fight against the negative forces.

Most of us don't even notice these things. We get up in the morning, go to the bathroom, eat our breakfast, go to our workplace, come back, do our other things and go to sleep. That's the life of most people. But a sadhak is not like that. A sadhak has to be very alert about everything that's going on, both outside and within his own mind. Amma's words are intended for people who want to become alert, who want to be careful and take advantage of everything for their spiritual progress.

Bhajan is a rajasic sadhana. It is a sadhana with a lot of activity in it. We are using our body, our voice, our mind, our feelings. We are not trying to become calm and quiet. Rather, we are trying to focus all of our being to one point, God.

Bhajan is not a sattvic sadhana because it is so active. Amma is saying that's what kind of sadhana is needed to fight the negative influences of the evening time. Sometimes it's good to fight fire with fire, and this is one instance of that.

"Children since the atmosphere in Kali Yuga is full of sounds, to get concentration, bhajan is better than meditation."

Just listen for a moment. Notice all the sounds. There is an airplane flying overhead, and a child is crying somewhere; there is a cow mooing, and somebody is opening and closing a door at the other end of the house. The birds are chirping and there are so many other sounds. This is something that is unavoidable. For a person whose mind is not strong, whose mind is not concentrated, any little sound becomes a disturbance when they try to meditate. So Amma says okay, we don't have to fight against the sounds; let us just drown them out with bhajan.

There was a funny incident in Amritapuri quite a long time ago. The ashramites were all sitting together one evening, when the neighbours, who were just about fifty feet away from us, started arguing. Well, argument would be an understatement; it was a war! They were screaming, shouting, throwing things; we just couldn't believe it. Never have I heard people fight like that; it was really an all out battle. And at that time, many people were coming to have Amma's darshan. Guess what she asked us to do? We had a small sound system; it was not a very high tech sound system. In fact, it was pretty bad. She said, "Turn it up full blast." So we put on a bhajan tape and blasted it so loud and distorted that you couldn't even hear what was on the tape! But at least we couldn't hear what was going on at the neighbours' house either. We couldn't hear anything but noise!

When I read this verse, I am reminded of that principle of Amma's. So, we can get beyond the noises by making even more noise. This is one reason why we do bhajan. Probably that did not occur to any of us; that's not why we are doing bhajan here, but it's one reason. If we try to meditate, our mind will be distracted by every little sound. But when we do bhajan, extraneous sound is not an element at all, as far as concentration or distraction goes. Of course, the reason we do bhajan is because our heart gets into that. Our heart opens up and we get more concentration at that time than at any other time in our lives. And so it is a very effective sadhana.

> "For meditation, quiet surroundings are necessary. For this reason, bhajan is more effective to gain concentration. With loud singing, other distracting sounds will be overcome and concentration will be achieved. Beyond concentration is meditation. Bhajan, concentration, meditation, this is the progression. Children, constant remembrance of God is meditation."

What is this *Kali Yuga* that Amma is talking about here? At the beginning of the verse, she said, "In the Kali Yuga, there are so many sounds." According to Indian philosophy, the Kali Yuga is a certain time period. Just as there are the Golden Age, Silver

Age, Copper Age and Iron Age with their different characteristics, the Kali Yuga is the age of discord. It is when materialism has its sway for a very long period of time.

There is a description the Kali Yuga which was written many thousands of years ago before it even started, by a sage, Vyasa Maharshi, who was describing what was going to happen in the future. When he wrote this description, things were not the way they are today, not by any means. The people were very dharmic minded. They were leading their life according to traditional ways. Their ideal was dharma, to follow their duty, to get the vision of God, to do good things all the time. A very well regulated life. So it's a wonder how accurate this mahatma was when he wrote this.

He's talking about the progression of time and he says about the Kali Yugas:

> "Thence forward, day after day, by force of the all-powerful Time, righteousness, purity of the mind and body, forgiveness, compassion, length of life, bodily strength, and keenness of memory will decline. In Kali Yuga, wealth alone will be the criterion of pedigree, and wealth alone will be the criterion of morality and merit. Again, might will be the only factor determining right. Personal liking will be the deciding factor in making a choice of a partner in life and trickery alone will be the motivating force in business dealings.

> "Justice will have every chance of being vitiated because of one's inability to gratify those administering it. Want of riches will be the sole test of impiety. And hypocrisy will be the only touchstone of goodness. Wearing long hair will be regarded as the only sign of beauty. Filling one's belly will be the only end of human pursuit. Skill will consist in supporting one's family. Virtuous deeds will be performed only with the object of gaining fame.

And when in this way, the terrestrial globe will be over-run by wicked people, the person who would prove to be the most powerful would become the ruler.

"Robbed of their wealth by greedy and merciless rulers behaving like robbers, people will resort to mountains and forests and subsist on leaves and roots, honey, fruits and flowers. Already oppressed by famine and taxation, people will perish through drought, cold, storms, sunshine, heavy rains, snowfall and mutual conflict. In the age of Kali, men will be tormented by hunger and thirst, ailments and worry, and their maximum age will only be twenty to thirty years."

This is not, of course, talking about right now. It is talking about from that time onwards till the end of the yuga; it will only get worse and worse. In the end, people will live only twenty or thirty years.

"When, through the evil effect of Kali, the bodies of men get reduced in size and emaciated, the righteous course chalked out by the Vedas gets lost. Then religion is replaced by heresy to a large extent and rulers mostly turn out to be thieves, when men take to various pursuits like theft, wanton destruction of life and so on, cows are reduced to the size of goats and begin to yield as much milk. Annual plants get stunted in growth, and trees are mostly reduced in size. Clouds will mostly end in flashes of lightning rather than pour rain. And dwellings will mostly look desolate for want of hospitality to strangers."

This is very interesting. Have you ever walked in a house that seemed so desolate that you would rather not be in there even though people are living in it? The reason is that there are bad vibrations there, usually due to the miserliness of the people who live there. They don't offer any hospitality to the people who come to their house. They just want to get rid of them as soon as possible in order to avoid having to feed them or give them something. Or maybe the people are always arguing in the house, so the vibrations are negative. Even though we don't know what the cause is, we can feel the effect. Likewise, if you go to a house where people regularly do bhajans and meditation, and they have satsang in the evenings, you'll feel peace their.

> "In this way, when the Kali Yuga whose career is so severe to the people is well nigh past, the Lord will appear for the protection of virtue."

At the end of Kali Yuga, they say that Lord Vishnu will take form as an avatar just as He had become the avatars Krishna and Rama. He will come again in the form of Kalki and make things much better. It will become the golden age, but that's not now. It's a very long time from now—about 432,000 years. And, of all the yugas, of all the ages, Kali is the shortest one. Our sense of time is not like God's sense of time. God's time is just like Mother Nature's time. We may plant a seed and then come out an hour later to see if it is sprouting, but that's not God's time. God will put the seed and sprout it accord to Nature's laws. It may take months, or it may take a whole year. It may take twenty years to get a tree and its fruits. So the yuga system is very vast from our standard of time.

> "If bhajan is sung without concentration, it is only a waste of energy. If sung with one-pointedness, it will be beneficial to the singer, the listener and also to nature. These songs will help awaken the listeners' minds in due course."

This is important, because bhajan is a very integral part of sadhana in Amma's presence and in her life and the lives of her devotees. We should do it with one-pointedness. When we sing, we should consciously try to concentrate our mind on one point.

That point may be anything. It may be between our eyes or it may be on a form, or it may be on a feeling or a light or anything that you want to concentrate on. But try to get your mind to a point, and, with all your feeling, try to merge your mind into that point and conceive of that as the Highest Truth. If a person does bhajan like that, or if we feel affected by listening to someone's bhajans, that's a sign that person is doing it with a lot of concentration. It has nothing to do with the quality or the tone of their voice. If a person is able to awaken other people spiritually with their singing, it's because their mind is so one-pointed.

Akbar and Tansen

In the sixteenth century, there was a great Indian musician called Tansen. He was the court musician for the Emperor Akbar. Unlike some other Mughal kings of the time, Akbar was not a fanatic. He was a broad-minded king and patronized all the different arts and religions. Tansen's music was fantastic. There was never a musician so great as Tansen. That's why he was considered to be one of the "jewels" in the court of Akbar.

One day, Akbar was thinking, 'As Tansen is so superb, what must his guru be like? I really want to hear his guru sing a song.'

He told Tansen, "I want to hear your guru sing once." What could Tansen say? He couldn't refuse. He's an employee after all. He said, "Okay, Maharaj." So they went to Brindavan to see his guru, Haridas Swami, who was living there. Brindavan is not very far from Delhi. It is a holy place in India just as Jerusalem is a holy place in the West. This is where Lord Krishna was born and lived for many years. There are many ashrams in there. So they went to his guru Haridas Swami's ashram. Even now we can go to that ashram and visit his tomb or samadhi. There is a holy presence and a deep peace in those environs.

Akbar had dressed up as a commoner. They walked in and bowed down to the swami. Haridas looked at Akbar and said, "Oh, the Emperor has come." He had immediately understood who Akbar was through his divine vision. Akbar kept making signs to Tansen to ask the guru to sing a song. Of course, it's not proper to ask a mahatma to sing songs. Tansen was very intelligent, so what did he do? He sang a song that Haridas had taught him, but he made some mistakes. So Haridas sang the same song in the correct way to show him how to sing it. When Akbar heard that song, he went into ecstasy.

The two of them took leave of Haridas and went back to Delhi. All the while, Akbar was thinking about the bliss that he experienced. He called Tansen the next day and said "Tansen, I can't forget the bliss I experienced yesterday. I want you to sing that song again for me." Tansen sang the same song, and Akbar just sat there with a straight face. When it was finished, he said, "I don't feel anything. What's the problem? It was the same song."

Tansen said, "Maharaj, if you don't get angry with me, I'll tell you what the problem is."

"Okay, tell me what it is."

"My guru was singing to please God. I am singing to please you."

Singing to please God is very different than singing to please an audience. Both may sound beautiful, but there is really no comparison. The difference is like that between day and night.

When we do bhajan, this should be our goal. We should have so much concentration that we'll get absorbed in God, and everybody around us also will feel that love and absorption in their heart.

Food and Sadhana - 1

"Without forsaking the taste of the tongue, the taste of the heart cannot be enjoyed."

THIS IS A VERY MYSTICAL EXPRESSION, AS ARE ALL of Amma's expressions. Food is very important. Life depends on food. If we look at the animal kingdom, most of life is spent searching for food, and the rest is in sleeping, mating, and looking after children. Most of us earn a living in order to eat and, secondarily, to live in and enjoy a house and other amenities. The main purpose of money is to stay alive through food. Many people spend hours cooking and cleaning up after cooking, and also going and purchasing things for cooking. Food is considered as a manifestation of God. Food is Brahman; this is what the Upanishads say. But Amma is saying that, even though nutritious food is important, taste is not the most important thing; it is not as important as the food itself. This verse is about taste and not food.

Man is not just a physical body that survives by food. He has five bodies, called *koshas* in Sanskrit. Just as an onion has rings around its center, the Atman or the "I", our real being, the soul, is covered by five layers or koshas.

The outermost layer is the gross physical body made of food. That's called the *annamaya kosha*, the kosha made of *annam* or food. Internal to that is the *pranamaya kosha*, the layer or sheath that's made of the life force or *prana*. Next comes the *manomaya kosha*, the part of us that's always thinking, feeling and perceiving—in other words, the mind. When the mind is used to discriminate, to understand, to decide, to make a decision, it's called the *vijnanamaya kosha* or the intellect. When we experience happiness, that happiness is actually not coming from outer objects but from the *anandamaya kosha* or the body of bliss. When we go into deep sleep without dreams, that blissful state is due to contact with the anandamaya kosha.

But the innermost being, the subject within and at the core of all these layers is the "I", the Atman. When the Atman leaves the body, the physical body is left behind, and the life force and mind are taken along to occupy the next body. Unfortunately, although we are always aware of the sense of "I", we mistake the five koshas for it due to proximity to them.

Amma says that the physical body, which is made of food, is not the most important thing in life. The most important thing is who we are—the "I", the Atman. But our sense life keeps our attention occupied almost all of the time.

As a result, we are quite unaware of that truth of the immortal bliss of our own Self—the Atman. Our mind is always directed to the outer world. Unless there is a certain amount of withdrawal from sense life, we can't perceive the taste of our real Self because we are completely immersed in the things outside.

Some people reach a stage in their spiritual evolution when they feel the emptiness and essence-less-ness of the world. They are just not satisfied with what's outside. Then they start to look inside. At that stage, they might experience something through association with someone like Amma. What do they experience? What is it that they are so intoxicated with? When people get up from Amma's lap, that look of bliss on their face is due to something that they are experiencing at that time. They got a glimpse of something.

At that time, if we would go over to them and say, "Hey, can you tell me what time it is?" they may not even look at us. They don't want to have to look outside. Even though their whole life is outside all the time, at that moment their mind is going deep within, and they taste the peace and bliss experienced due to Amma's presence. Even during a good bhajan, if somebody knocks against you and says, "Shall we go outside and have a talk?" you won't even look at them. Why? Because the mind is going beyond the physical body, beyond the life force, beyond thinking, beyond the intellect. It is touching the Self; it is getting near to the inner reality. When we start to experience that, then we feel as if our sense life has become a distraction. The experience of inner peace can be obtained through the grace of a mahatma. Through a certain amount of sense control and meditation also, we can experience that.

If we always look outside, we cannot experience the bliss inside. Amma says that the bliss is in the heart, meaning not the physical heart, but the core of one's being, the place where the Atman resides. There is a saying: "Where there is Rama, there is no kama, and where there is kama, there is no Rama." What does it mean? Kama means desire, or you could say worldly enjoyment. So, where worldly enjoyments are and when desire is, at that moment, we cannot talk about the presence of God. They are two opposite ends of the pendulum. When we are talking about or experiencing God, at that moment there can be no desire or external worldly enjoyment.

> "It is not possible to definitely say that a particular thing can or cannot be eaten. Depending on climatic conditions, the influence of the diet on us will also be changing. The types of food avoided here may be useful in the Himalayas."

According to realized people like Amma and the ancient *rishis*, this world has a dual nature; there is the physical world and the world of subtle vibrations. Thousands of years ago, the ancient sages sensed that everything radiates a vibration and receives vibrations also. Not only human beings, but also everything in existence is sending and receiving—places, foods, thoughts, actions, words—they all have vibrations. The whole universe is a vast network, a vast matrix of ever-changing vibrations, all based on a vibrationless substratum, which is called God or Brahman.

These vibrations are basically divided into three categories called gunas. Many of us might have read the philosophy of the gunas as explained in the Bhagavad Gita.

Gunas in Actions and People

"An action which is ordained, which is free from attachment, which is done without love or hatred by one not desirous of the fruit, that action is sattvic."

—Ch.18, v.23

In other words, an action performed when one is not attached to the results and one is balanced and calm, that kind of action is sattvic karma, sattvic action.

"But the action which is done by one longing for pleasure or done by the egotist, which causes much trouble, that is declared to be rajasic.

"The action that is undertaken from delusion, from mistakenness, without regarding the consequences, loss, injury and inability, that is declared to be tamasic."

—Ch.18, v.24-25

This means that when our mind is over active and full of desire, or covered with dullness and doesn't take into consideration all that it should, that is a rajasic or tamasic action.

Now we are talking about people.

"Free from attachment, not given to egotism, endued with firmness and vigour, unaffected in success and failure, such a person is said to be sattvic."

"Passionate, desiring to attain the fruit of action, greedy, cruel, impure, subject to joy and sorrow, such a person is said to be rajasic."

—Ch.18, v.26-27

Most people in the world are rajasic. Not many people are sattvic—sattvic people are free of attachment, have no egotism, and are balanced in success and failure. How many of us are like that? But that is what we should be aiming for. The closer we get to the sattvic nature, the closer we are getting to our real Self, the Atman.

"Uncultured, vulgar, arrogant, deceitful, malicious, indolent, slothful, and procrastinating, such a person is said to be tamasic."

—Ch.18, v.28

Importance of the Mind

When Amma is saying that different foods should or shouldn't be eaten, she's not talking about what is good or bad for health. There are plenty of people that can tell us that; it's a big industry. But not everybody knows what is good or bad for us spiritually, like what should be eaten for our spiritual good so as to increase the quality of sattva in us, and what to avoid so as not to become more rajasic and tamasic. Very few people are concerned about that at all except spiritual aspirants. Spiritual aspirants are more concerned about their mind than their body. They know that the body is perishable, and might fall off at any moment. We may walk out the door, and that will be the last anybody will see of us. The breath that goes out may never come in again. As soon as we are born, we are put in the queue, we have our ticket to go—to leave the world—but we don't know the date of departure.

The body is here today and gone tomorrow. But the mind is the most important thing, more important than the body, because the mind will continue even after death and on into the next birth. Whatever body we may get, the same mind will be there. And the more sattvic the mind is, the closer we will be to perceiving the Atman. And then this unfortunate matter of being born and dying again and again will be over. It will be like waking up from a very long, bad dream. The bliss that we are always looking for in this world—we will find it in that state, we will find it in our own Self. We will finally be home. So it is most important that we purify our mind, make our mind sattvic.

While living in this world of vibrations, we should try to eat only sattvic things.

What is sattvic food? The Bhagavad Gita says:

"The food also which is dear to each person is three fold. Foods which increase life, energy, strength, health, joy and cheerfulness, which are savoury and oleaginous, substantial and agreeable, are dear to the sattvic people. Foods that are bitter, sour, salty, excessively hot, pungent, dry and burning, are loved by the rajasic, causing pain, grief and disease. Food which is stale, tasteless, putrid, rotten and impure is dear to the tamasic."

—Ch. 17, v. 7-10

Don't laugh! One can tell to a great degree which guna predominates in people by what they like to eat.

Sometimes the guna of a thing may change according to climate. For example, take tea. Tea in a hot climate like in south India is rajasic; it's a strong stimulant. But if we live in Tibet where it's very cold, we have to drink tea if we want to survive. Also, they don't have many vegetables there, so the main staple is barley with dairy and meat. Meat is generally considered tamasic, but in Tibet, it is what gives you life.

Having this in mind, Amma is saying you can't definitely say a particular food is good or bad; it changes according to the climate.

What's good may have to be avoided there and vice versa. But in general, these categories apply. We should try to learn what is sattvic, what is rajasic, what is tamasic and try to limit ourselves to what is sattvic. That is, of course, if we are really serious about making spiritual progress.

Amma's words will be taken to heart by serious aspirants. To those for whom spiritual life is a hobby or a part time interest, the absolute seriousness of them may not be clear. But for those who feel, 'I may die any day, and I haven't experienced my Self, I haven't really attained happiness. What is the solution? I'm going to get old, I'm going to get sick, I'm going to die; all these are going to happen to me too, not just to others. Isn't there some way out?', her words will be a beacon in the darkness of the ocean of birth and death.

Everyone knows the story of Buddha. At first, he had thought his life was going along great; it would be a festival till the end, and he would always be young and healthy. Then what happened? When he went outside of the palace grounds, he saw old people, sick people, those who were dying and the dead. He also saw a holy man. When he asked his attendant, "Is this just for them that these things happen or is it going to happen to me too?"

Then Channa, his attendant, said, "Everybody gets sick, everybody gets old, everybody dies—even you, even your wife Yasodhara, even the king—everybody."

Then he said, "I feel sick, take me back to the palace." He started thinking, 'What is the way to escape from this? I don't want to go through that; that's horrible.' Then he thought about the sadhu who was sitting under the tree. He was meditating, trying to escape from the inevitable. So he decided, 'This is the way for me,' and he left.

I'm not saying that we all have to leave everything and go and sit under a tree and meditate until we attain Enlightenment.

That is not the point. Seriousness means to look at the way life is—not only the pleasant side but also the painful side—and not to get lost in Maya, to see the seriousness of our situation and the necessity of spiritual life. If that's not there, at least think what you got from Amma's presence, or the satsang; what about the bliss, the joy, the peace, that unique feeling you got in Amma's presence when she was here, when spiritual life became a reality instead of just a hobby?

These words are for such serious people.

Control of Hunger

> "When one sits to eat food, one should proceed only after praying to God. This is why a mantra is chanted before eating. The proper time to test our patience is when food is in front of us."

This is a spiritual practice. In other words, to sit still even though our mouth may be watering, and think of God. It's a great tapas; it's an austerity. It's very difficult, when something is right in front of us that we want to enjoy, and we think, 'No, wait a minute, I am going to think about God or meditate first.' That is the time to do it. One's character is tested in the face of hunger. We can really tell what a person is when they are hungry. It's said that even some saintly devotees may throw away everything for the sake of their belly. The urge of hunger is such a powerful urge.

Many of us may have read the story of Kuchela, the devotee of Krishna. When he and Krishna were young men, they were sent out into the forest to collect wood for their guru, and the guru's wife had given them a packet of something to eat so that while they were out there they would have a little snack. But unfortunately, it started raining cats and dogs. They got stuck out there and couldn't get back, so they took shelter in the trees. Krishna was in one tree and Kuchela was in another tree. Kuchela started feeling very hungry. He knew Krishna was Bhagavan, he knew Krishna was Lord Vishnu. Even then, he started eating without asking Krishna if He wanted some. The food was getting less and less, and even when it was beyond the fifty-percent mark—his share—he continued and ate the whole thing. For many years after that, he lived a life of poverty. Finally, Krishna came to see him when he was an old man in order to bless him with the wealth he wanted. This story shows us that, even though he had the company of God, his belly had got the better of him.

I had an experience like that. I kind of feel shy about it, but I feel that it may be of some value to others, and that's why I'm writing this. I was serving an elderly sadhu who had an acidity problem, so he couldn't eat yogurt unless it had no acidity. I was not sick but I also liked yogurt before it turned sour.

This person had gone to a temple and said he would come back for lunch and so I arranged his food. When I opened the cupboard, I found that there were two little pots of yogurt. One was very sour; one was sweet. Well, he didn't know that there were two. So, before he got back, I gobbled down the sweet one. Even with all my respect for him—I was serving this person—taste had gotten the better of me. My stomach, my tongue—they got the better of me. What used to always happen at that stage of my life was that, whenever I had made a big mistake, I would get clobbered on the head in the next minute.

He soon came and ate his lunch, and while eating the sour yogurt, he said, "Hey, this is so sour! Wasn't there any sweet yogurt here?" So I had to admit what I had done.

He said, "That's very nice, you are a great sadhak, a great devotee."

Of course, he was not Bhagavan Sri Krishna, so I didn't have to suffer too much for it, but I learned a life long lesson not to do that, and to be aware of how the tongue makes us its slave, and we end up throwing away our discrimination.

Then there is the story from the Mahabharata of the golden mongoose, wherein the great Pandava king, Yudhisthira, performed a big Vedic sacrifice, and gave away millions of rupees. He gave many gifts away to thousands of people; it had been the talk of Hastinapura (the present day Delhi). At the end of this sacrifice, a mongoose came and rolled in the dirt where the ceremony had been performed. Everybody saw this and wondered, 'What a strange creature this is'. When it got up, they noticed that one side of the body was a beautiful golden color, and the other side was its normal brown color. So one of them asked the mongoose, "You're the strangest looking mongoose. How did you get gold on half your body?" The mongoose then told a story.

"Some years ago, when I had been wandering around the country looking for something to eat, there was a terrible famine. I came upon a poor family, who were about to die from starvation. Somehow, they found a bit of wheat, and, powdering it into flour, made a few chappatis. They were just about to eat. Just imagine their hunger: they hadn't eaten for about two or three weeks; they were trembling and about to collapse, and there must have been a raging fire in their stomachs. And then, they were about to get three or four pieces of bread...

"Just at that time, three guests arrived, one after another. They gave one piece of bread to each guest. Finally, there was nothing left to give. At that moment, when they were willing to sacrifice their all, God suddenly liberated them from *samsara* and took their souls to His world.

"I then went over to eat the crumbs that had fallen down from the mouth of the guests. After eating, I lay there for a moment, and when I got up, half of my body was golden. I was so enamoured of the gold color that I wanted to get the other half to also match. So I used to go to all the great places of pilgrimage where people were doing puja, charity, selfless service and other meritorious acts. Then I would roll on the ground there and see if the other side had become golden."

Looking at the king, he said, "This great ceremony in which you gave away millions of rupees and so many gifts is nothing compared to those people who only gave away three pieces of bread."

This shows the greatness of being able to control hunger. Only a great person can do that.

> "An ascetic need not wander in search of food. The spider weaves its web and remains in its place. It does not go anywhere searching for food. Its prey will get entangled in its web. Likewise, the food for an ascetic will come to him through God, but he must be a man of total surrender to God."

We are talking about a real sannyasi, not about most of us. Such a person, who has left everything of the worldly life and lives only for God-realization, should not even think about food or where it is going to come from. They need not make any effort. If they are making effort all the time to realize God, the food has to come to them. Another mahatma said the same thing two thousand years ago:

> "Therefore I tell you, do not worry about your life, what you will eat or drink; or about your body, what you will wear. Is not life more than food, and the body more than clothes? Look at the birds of the air; they do not sow or reap or store away in barns, and yet your heavenly Father feeds them. Are you not much more valuable than they? So do not worry, saying, 'What shall we eat?' or 'What shall we drink?' or 'What shall we wear?' But seek first

his kingdom and his righteousness, and all these things will be given to you as well."

—Jesus Christ, New Testament, Matthew

God Looks After His Devotees

Amma tells a story about a man who heard this teaching at a satsang and decided he was going to test it to see whether God was really going to feed him if he didn't make any effort. He thought, 'Not only should God bring the food to me, but God should put it in my mouth also; then only I will believe.' So he went into the forest and sat under a tree doing his mantra.

After some time, he heard a band of thieves coming his way. He thought, 'They may kill me!', so he climbed up into the tree. When the robbers came, they put down the bags of the things they had stolen, and then took out their lunch. One of them said, "Let's go and take a bath in the river nearby and then enjoy our lunch."

So they left the place and came back after bathing. Just at that time, the man in the tree sneezed; he couldn't help himself. The thieves looked up and saw him. They said, "Hey, you. Come down here!"

Then the leader thought, 'He saw all this stuff that we stole. He must have come down when we went to the river and poisoned our food to make sure that we will all die and then he will take everything.' So he decided they would make him eat the food. They pushed it into his mouth until he couldn't eat any more.

At that moment, the man realized that what he heard in satsang about God was true. Of course, the police came into the forest and took the thieves away, and this man lived happily ever after, all the wiser for it.

Be a Good Example

"In the initial stages, a sadhak should exercise control with respect to food. Uncontrolled diet will produce bad tendencies. Once seeds are sown, care should be taken not to let crows peck them. After the seed has grown into a tree, any bird can sit on it or build a nest there. Now itself, our diet should be controlled and sadhana should be done. At a later stage, pungent and spicy food can be eaten and it won't effect you. Children, just because Amma told you that at a later stage such food can be eaten, don't eat those foods even then. You should live as a model to the world. Then others will learn by observing you. Don't eat spicy and fried foods in front of a person affected by jaundice. Even though we don't have the disease ourselves, we should exercise self-control in order to make others good."

A patient came to see a doctor, who examined him and said, "You have diabetes," but didn't give him a prescription. He told the man, "Come back tomorrow."

The man said, "Sir, I have come a long distance to see you. Please give me a prescription so that I can return home today."

"Sorry, I can't give you any prescription now, so you please come back tomorrow."

The man left.

The nurse said, "Doctor, how cruel you are. Why didn't you give him the prescription and directions about his diet?"

"Don't you see this bowl of candies on my desk? If I had said to him, "Don't eat sugar, don't eat candy," then he would have thought, 'He's telling me not to eat candy and sugar but *he* is eating candy and sugar,' and he may not follow my advice."

Amma is saying that we may have reached a stage where the fire of *jñana* or wisdom may be shining in our hearts; we may be living in the presence of God. In that case, whatever we eat won't affect our mind. But ordinary people are not like that; their minds are influenced by what they eat. They may look up to us as a role model; so, for their sake, we should be a good example even in matters of what we eat. The Bhagavad Gita says:

> "Whatsoever a great man does, that alone other men do. Whatever he sets up as a standard, the world follows. I have nothing whatsoever to achieve in the three worlds, nor is there anything unattained that should be attained by Me, yet, I engage in action. For, should I not ever engage in action, men would in all matters follow My path. These worlds would be ruined if I should not perform action. I should be the cause of confusion and destroy all these creatures. As ignorant men act attached to work, so should the wise act unattached from a wish to protect the masses. Let no wise man cause unsettlement in the minds of the ignorant who are attached to action. He should make them do all actions, himself fulfilling them with devotion."
>
> —Ch. 3, v. 21-26

A wise person, a God-realized Soul, may be beyond all the rules and regulations of society and scripture. Yet, for the sake of the world, to set an example, they should lead an ideal life.

Amma needs no rules or regulations. Before any of us came, she used to live out in the sun and the rain. She cared for nothing. But when the world started to come to her, she adapted, in her external life, to the norms of society. For what reason? Only in order to set an example, to guide the people whom God brought to her. She is the picture of self-sacrifice and compassion.

Food and Sadhana - 2

EVEN THOUGH AMMA TALKS SPECIFICALLY ABOUT food that goes into the mouth, spiritually speaking, food has to be considered as everything that goes into us through our sense organs. What we hear, what we see, what we smell, what we taste, what we touch, all are composed of the three gunas or qualities of Nature.

Most of us are completely externalized. We are identifying only with the outermost sheath of our existence, the body, although we may be conscious of the other four sheaths. There is nobody who is unconscious of the Self. The only thing is that we mix it up with the other sheaths. We are unable to separate the "I" from its appendages, and that is what spiritual life is all about—trying to separate the external from the innermost essential thing, the core, the Atman or soul. We are not a body that has a soul but rather a soul that has a body.

Here is Amma's verse:

> "One will say that to stop drinking tea or to quit smoking is easy, yet, one is unable to do it. How is it possible for someone to control his mind if he cannot even control these simple things? First these simple things should be curtailed. If one cannot cross small rivers, how then to cross the ocean?"

Amma is clearly saying here that drinking tea—under the heading of tea we could include stimulants, anything that is other than nourishing to the body, that stimulates the nervous system—and smoking are not good for us if we are serious about spiritual life. Why? Because we already have enough restlessness and wandering of the mind, and spiritual life means trying to concentrate the mind, trying to get peace of mind.

Peace of mind doesn't come from comfort, or wealth or pleasant situations. That's only a temporary peace that's dependent on circumstance. Peace of mind is the absence of thought and that can be gained only by culturing the mind through spiritual practice. Suppose we want to build up a muscle; the muscle is not going to come by itself. We have to practice. We have to lift heavy weights, gradually increasing them more and more. In the same way, peace of mind is not the birthright of anybody; it's the fruit of hard work. That is what meditation is about, that is what bhajan is about, that is what satsang is about. It needs a conscious effort. If we have decided that peace of mind is worth the effort, that it is the real purpose of life, then we have got to enquire what all the means are, what all the aids are to attaining that.

For such a person who is serious about it—not for somebody for whom it is just a hobby or a part time business, but somebody who has decided that's the purpose of life and whatever else I may do, I am going to achieve that, I'm going to try to get my mind to stop wandering and to become completely still and calm—for such a person, Amma is laying down all these rules by making these suggestions.

Tea, coffee, anything that stimulates the nerves is not good because it contributes to restlessness of mind. We may think, 'Well, what does it matter? When I sit to meditate I won't drink tea or coffee.' But meditation, or sitting for meditation, is only the beginning of spiritual life. That is only beginner's stuff. We have to do that a couple of times a day to get into the habit. But there should be a constant effort at trying to restrain the wandering mind. That is real spiritual life. That is meditation. Drinking tea and coffee will stimulate our mind at other times also and make it hard to control it. Smoking clogs the nervous system. Of course, everybody knows that it's bad for health. But Amma is not concerned about that in this particular discussion. She does say certain things about what is good and bad for health, but her main concern is about our mind and our spirit, and not so much about our body. Our body is here today and will be gone tomorrow, but the mind is eternal, that will go on for a much longer time, until we realize our true nature, the Atman. Amma says that smoking clogs the nervous system and makes our mind tamasic or dull. It makes it difficult to concentrate, to understand, to make effort. Smoking is a tamasic habit.

Some people who lead a spiritual life say, "I can give up tea and coffee," but they don't. They feel, 'What does it matter, after all?' If it doesn't matter, then why indulge? Amma is saying, "If it is difficult doing that, what to say of the real work?" That means, giving up a physical habit is not the real work; it is only the prep work. The hard stuff is giving up internal habits.

There is a principle in nature that the subtle is stronger than the gross, that the gross has its source in the subtle. It is much more powerful. In the same way, it is our mind that is much more powerful than our physical habits. In fact, they come into existence because of our mind. The body is just an inert thing. It is an instrument of the mind. It has no will of its own.

The vast ocean of inner enemies are much more difficult to cross than a few small rivers like smoking and drinking. And what are the inner enemies? There are six main ones. In fact, they are enemies for everyone. Though we are talking about spiritual life, spiritual life doesn't mean going away and renouncing everything and becoming a monk. Spiritual life is human life. It's necessary for everybody in order to succeed and to be happy. Spirituality is a necessity. It's not even a choice. Ultimately, all beings come to it.

What are these six enemies? Kama, desire; *krodha*, anger; *lobha*, greed; *moha*, attachment; *mada*, pride, and *matsarya*, jealousy. These are the six enemies that keep coming up and causing so much trouble for us. These are the things that will always distract us. They will always cause conflict in our lives. So we have to remember them.

The mind is very complex. Mahatmas like Bhagavan Sri Krishna analysed it down to its essence, and found that these are the big troublemakers. These are the hoodlums, you could say—the Mafia of the mind. If we catch them, if we put them in jail, then everything will be all right.

It's worth repeating what they are, but we will leave off the Sanskrit this time: desire, anger, greed, attachment, pride, jealousy. Each one is like an ocean. We might think we got rid of one, but it comes up again and again. We think, 'I never get angry,' and then somebody says something that we don't like and we get angry. We think we are beyond all desire and temptation but we immediately fall a prey to that. We may think we are very detached, but when somebody leaves us or mistreats us, we feel miserable. Our life depended upon that relationship or that person. We may think that we have no greed, but we look at a thing wishing that it were ours, thinking, 'Oh, that is a nice thing,' instead of being satisfied with what we have.

Vishwamitra Maharishi's Tapas

Vishwamitra was a king. One day, he went with his army to Vasishta Maharshi's ashram. The Maharshi was a *Brahmarishi*, a brahmin sage who had attained God-realization. Vishwamitra was a *kshatriya*, a member of the warrior caste.

Vasishta fed Vishwamitra a sumptuous meal along with his vast army. Vishwamitra was thinking, 'Where is he getting all this delicious food and all these provisions from in this little ashram out in the forest?'

He asked Vasishta, "Where has all this food come from? I don't even see a cook. After all, we just came half an hour ago and you served us a ten-course meal. Your wife is a ninety year old lady, so she could not have done all this."

Vasishta replied, "I have a magic cow that gives anything we ask. Not just milk, but also all products will come out ready made. She is like a fast food machine. She is like the legendary wish-fulfilling tree."

Vishwamitra wanted to see this cow. He saw her and said, "Listen, a sadhu like you, a poor sage in the forest, doesn't need a cow like this. This would be a great thing for me. I'm a king. I have got to feed thousands of people in the palace every day and we need so many provisions and other things. This cow is overkill for you. You can get everything but you don't need anything. So, I want the cow."

"No, I'm sorry I can't give you the cow because I need it for my puja," said Vasishta. "She gives me milk every day and I use the milk and the yogurt and the ghee for my daily worship."

Then Vishwamitra got angry and shouted, "I don't care; I'm taking the cow," and tried to take it away.

There was a big fight. Between whom? Between Vishwamitra and his army on one side, and Vasishta on the other side. Poor old Vasishta was probably about a hundred and twenty-five years old at that time. But he's got the cow on his side. So the cow manifested soldiers instead of food and the fight was on. Vishwamitra was defeated and he went back to his country. He decided, "That is real power. That poor brahmin, he's really got power, spiritual power. What's the use of being a king? I want to become a brahmarishi like him. I'll do meditation. I'll do tapas, penance."

So he went to the forest and was doing penance. What happened? In the meantime, Indra, the king of the gods, saw

Vishwamitra doing tapas and thought, 'Why is he doing tapas? He probably wants to get my position, he wants to become the king of heaven.' So he sent down a beautiful lady named Menaka. She was a celestial damsel, a nymph. She distracted Vishwamitra with her feminine charms, and, as a result, they became lovers. For how long? Twelve years! He didn't know how the time passed; it had seemed like a day. They also had a child, Sakuntala. After twelve years, he realized what had happened, that he had forgotten his meditation and tapas. He understood that Indra must have done this mischief, so he got very angry and cursed Menaka.

Again, he sat down for tapas. But because he had wasted all his energy with Menaka, and on top of that, had gotten angry, all the benefit that he had gotten from those previous years of meditation was gone. He felt pretty miserable and thought, 'Look what happened to me. I fell prey to desire, anger and greed. Never again will I let this thing happen to me.'

He went to another place and sat for meditation again. Again, Indra sent another lady. She distracted him also, but he decided that he was at least not going to get angry. He didn't curse her. One thing after another was happening like this. He couldn't get over his anger.

That was the big problem for him, even in spite of so much of meditation and tapas. He stood on one toe for fifty years. He took one breath of air once in a year for his food. He never slept day or night. He stood out in the rain and the sun. Even then, when a problem would come up, he would get angry. He couldn't control his anger try as he may. The worst part was that, in spite of everything, Vasishta would not accept him as a brahmarishi.

Finally, he couldn't bear it any more. He decided that he was going to kill Vasishta. He became so jealous and angry. He said, "If this is the only way that I can defeat him and get his position, it is worth killing him." His mind got so perverted. So he went to the ashram one full moon night. He hid behind a hut and waited to finish off Vasishta.

At that time, Vasishta was giving a talk, a satsang. He told the brahmacharis and *brahmacharinis* in the ashram, "You see the beautiful moon in the sky, how it gives light to the whole world and makes everybody so happy and peaceful and cools down the heat of the day. In the same way, that great mahatma who is doing tapas in the forest, that Vishwamitra, gives peace to the world."

When Vishwamitra heard that, all his anger was dissipated. He became like an innocent child. He repented for all the bad things that he had done and went and fell at the feet of Vasishta. He held onto Vasishta's feet. Vasishta said, "Get up, Brahmarishi, get up! Why are you lying down? You are a brahmarishi, not because of your tapas but because your heart has become pure and childlike."

This is, ultimately, the only way our mind will become completely pure. To get rid of these deep-rooted vasanas, these oceans of vasanas, we have to do spiritual practice.

But, ultimately, it depends on a mahatma's grace, just like Vishwamitra got Vasishta's grace. We may feel that it is impossible to do, but I personally saw something that happened that shows that we can conquer such habits.

There was a scientist living in Mumbai who used to drink about thirty cups of coffee a day. He used to chew betel leaves, a kind of stimulant—maybe twenty packages of betel leaves and nuts a day. He was getting a pretty good salary in those days and, except for his rent money, he spent the entire salary on coffee, betel leaves and the little food that he was eating. He was never really very hungry because of eating and drinking all those things. It would be an understatement to say that he was wired as if a powerful electric current was going through him all the time.

But, at the same time, he was very attached to Amma. He came to Amma and said, "I want to leave my old life. I want to live at your feet, Amma." Amma said, "Okay, but I will let you stay here only if you can give up these two habits"

Well, it was a struggle for him and he succeeded only for a few days. Then he went to Amma and said, "Amma, I can't control myself."

She said, "There is no wonder in that. You eat some sugar candy whenever you feel the urge to drink coffee or chew betel." So he was eating lots of sugar candy. He was sick of sugar candy. He was over saturated with sugar candy. But that didn't do the trick.

One day, he left the ashram and went to a teashop and got some coffee and a packet of betel nuts and leaves. Nobody told Amma; nobody even knew. He had done it on the sly. It must have been at night or when everybody was meditating. But his mind was on the coffee and so he went out to have darshan of the tea shop.

When he came back, Amma called him and said, "You can't fool me, I know what you did. I told you that, if you can't conquer those habits, you can't stay here."

He felt so bad about this, to the core of his being, that from that day onwards, he never touched coffee or betel leaves again. A habit that was so deep rooted was he kicked then and there. He had a deep conviction that, 'This is not good for me and I can't get Amma's grace if I persist in this.' So when that got all the way into his heart, not just in his head, then he was able to remove that habit once and for all.

So it is possible. But always remember that Amma says that if we can't conquer even these habits, how are we going to conquer the oceans of anger and negative qualities in the mind?

Power of Thought

Now, here is something that may sound a little strange here in the Western world, but we should hear it from Amma.

"In the beginning, a sadhak, a spiritual aspirant, should not eat anything from shops."

You could say restaurants instead of shops.

"While taking each and every ingredient, the shop-keeper's only thought will be how to make more profit. When making tea, he will think, "Is this much milk needed? Why can't the sugar be reduced?" In this way he will only have thoughts to reduce the quantity to gain more profit. The vibration of these thoughts will affect the sadhak."

Here in the Western world, and more and more all over the world, social life is very important. Restaurants are never thought of as a place not to go. In fact, almost everybody who has the money goes out to eat. I read somewhere that McDonald's sells about 6,480,000 hamburgers in a day worldwide. This works out to seventy-five hamburgers every second!

Log ago, there weren't restaurants in India. There might have been inns for travellers. There were, and still are, *dharamsalas* and *annasatras*, where people on pilgrimage could rest and have something to eat. These would be maintained freely by wealthy communities—probably the traders and merchants.

It's true that the food in your home that is cooked with love is good for you spiritually. It's good for your body; it's good for your mind. The food in restaurants is not good for your mind. It's cooked only with the idea of making a profit. We should remember that it's a business. It is not out of love that they're feeding you.

Amma tells a story about a father and his little daughter who checked into a hotel. The next morning, they were checking out and the little girl said, "Daddy, the staff here were so nice! For every little thing, they were rushing about to please us, and so many people were serving us in the restaurant also, asking us again and again, 'Do you want anything else?' They were so loving and kind. I have never seen such wonderful and sweet people."

Then the father said, "What are you talking about? After I pay the bill, you won't even see them. The only reason they are so sweet and kind is to get our money. That's just a façade—a show. If you don't pay the bill, you will see how sweet they are!"

A restaurant, however nice the employees and the atmosphere may be, however delicious the food may seem to taste, is not good spiritually. The subtle part of that food, which is the vibration that enters our mind, creates tendencies of wanting profit instead of wanting to give to become more selfless and sharing—because that greediness lodges in our mind.

That was the first half of the verse. Then Amma tells a little story.

> "There was a sannyasi who was not in the habit of reading newspapers. One day, an intense desire to read the newspaper sprang up in him. Afterwards, he started dreaming about newspapers and about the news. Upon enquiring, it was discovered that the servant was reading the newspaper while cooking his lunch. His attention was not on the cooking but on reading the newspaper. The thought waves of the cook affected the sannyasi."

When we're cooking, our thoughts, our vibrations, are going into the food. It is not so with a raw thing like a banana or something uncooked. Ancient Indian tradition and mahatmas like Amma say that food becomes sensitive to vibrations after being cooked. Whoever handles it, their vibrations go into the food. In a house where there is affection, that will go into the food and will nourish the people's minds. But in a hotel or a restaurant, there is nothing like that, and those worldly vibrations will go into the food.

Amma says it is best, in the beginning of our sadhana, to not eat anything from restaurants or shops. We don't have to follow this rule forever. But most of us are only beginners in spiritual life. Even if we've been meditating for twenty years, seen every mahatma that ever came to America, been to India forty times and to every single ashram, and stood on our head for so many hours, still, we haven't got a hold of our mind yet. It still wanders and wanders like the wind. So, until the mind has a real, permanent peace that is not disturbed by anything, until we feel inner bliss without any external cause, until we reach that stage of spiritual evolution, we are affected by everything. A serious sadhak has to be careful. However unnatural it may seem, however difficult it may seem, it's for our good.

If we are not serious, we can do whatever we like; there's no problem.

Eat with Moderation

"Don't eat food until you suffocate. Half the stomach should be for food, a quarter for water and the remaining for the movement of air."

This is, of course, an ideal. I've never met a person who could follow this. It's very hard to eat a half stomach worth of food. Still, we have to know about the highest ideal. This is an Ayurvedic principle.

"The less food eaten, the more mental control there will be. Do not sleep or meditate immediately after eating. Otherwise proper digestion will not take place."

Here's a healthy advice. Don't eat so much that we are about to burst. I saw a cow once in the ashram. Nobody knew how much it had eaten, and we didn't know at that time that cows could eat themselves to death. This cow was given more and more food. A person saw the empty bucket and thought, 'Poor cow, it hasn't been given any food.' So two or three people were feeding the cow. It became so full that it almost exploded and died of indigestion.

Some people are like that. A thing is so tasty that they just go on eating long after their hunger is over. Then, if we bring something to them, something they like, then suddenly they have some more room to eat. I've seen it many times. Payasam (pudding), that's a favourite of many people. We've eaten a ten course Indian meal, and are about to burst, when somebody comes with some more rice and vegetables, or *sambar* or *rasam,* and they say, "Would you like some more rice?"

"No, no, I am so full, it's up to here."

Then somebody comes and says, "You haven't had any payasam."

"Oh, all right, I'll have some payasam."

It must have been coming out of their ears by that time. Everybody can find some room when it's something they like.

We shouldn't eat to the point where we can't even breathe, because we will become very tamasic. We know what happens when we eat too much food. We snooze. That's good if we want to go to sleep, but it's not good if we want to meditate. Amma says we shouldn't sleep or meditate after eating a full meal. Why? Because, if we sleep, we don't get proper digestion, and as a result, we don't get proper nourishment and may even get indigestion, and the next day, we'll get acidity. And, if we meditate, what will happen? Same thing, because when we meditate, our life force that digests the food, will be channeled to the point on which we are meditating. We don't want to deprive our stomach of its natural processes. So don't meditate after eating a full meal. Wait for an hour or two.

This is the last verse in that chapter:

"Once love for God develops, it is similar to a person suffering from fever. The person affected by fever will not find any taste in food. Even though it may be sweet, the food will taste bitter. Once we have love for God, the appetite spontaneously decreases."

This is the final word. For some time, it may be a struggle to control these natural urges so that we can get a glimpse of something higher than sense happiness or sense experience. It will be a struggle, no doubt, because we've had many births of living like that. But once we get real spiritual experience, once we taste the presence of God or the Self, it becomes natural. Then we don't feel like looking for anything outside ourselves; those things no longer make us happy. Sense life becomes an unavoidable distraction, a waste of time. When we start to relish spiritual practice, physical life becomes tasteless. We will feel that sleeping, cooking, eating, bathing and going to the toilet are such a waste of time.

After Mental Control, Bliss Comes

Spiritual life is a life of bliss and inner peace. It may become a life of suffering and misery for a time only. We have heard the expression, "The dark night of the soul." That happens at the beginning of a truly spiritual life. At that time, the habits that we had picked up from society, our family and other worldly associations, surface with great intensity and we become acutely aware of them. We feel very bad and try to get rid of them, but the task feels hopeless.

People who see us going around with a long face may say, "I thought you were a spiritual person; you're supposed to be radiant with divine bliss."

Nobody gets a college degree without first going through the entire school system from kindergarten to the university. How can we experience bliss without passing through the dark night of the soul? A certain degree of purity must be achieved through concentration, other spiritual sadhanas, and the fight with our negativities before peace begins to dawn. In fact, it is a sign that we are on the right track if this upheaval happens.

The grossest vasanas or habits we indulged in, not only in this lifetime, but also in our past lifetimes, will come up first. Selfishness, lust, anger, stinginess, jealousy and fault-finding are some of the "popular" ones. But once we make a dent in those, the scum on the surface of the pond of the mind moves aside for a moment and we see some clear water. Once we start to get a glimpse of our real nature, the Atman, or we start to feel the presence of God, or feel some devotion, then spiritual life becomes easier and eventually, natural.

Amma says, "First comes the rehearsal; then the real play starts."

Sadhana is like a rehearsal and the state of bliss is like the play.

I'd like to read just a few things that are describing the experience of someone who attained bliss, because it's very rare that we find descriptions of that. There are a lot of people in the present day and age who write about their experiences. This is somebody who went to a Guru in a traditional way a couple thousand years ago and took refuge in the Guru, was trained by the Guru, and then experienced Divine Bliss. This is his description:

"Having understood the supreme truth on the authority of the scriptures, the instruction by the Guru and by his own reasoning, with his senses stilled and the mind controlled, the disciple became motionless in a lonely place. Establishing his mind for a while in Brahman, the Supreme Reality, he got up and spoke as follows out of the abundance of his joy."

He steadied his mind, went to a quiet place, all alone, made his mind completely still and thought about the teachings that he had studied and everything that his Guru had told him. His mind became one-pointed and it experienced supreme bliss.

Then he said, "The magnificence of the ocean of the Supreme Brahman filled with the nectar of realization of the Self, cannot be adequately expressed in words, nor thought of by the mind. My mind, which has attained such a state, and merged in that ocean, is now content by the enjoyment of bliss. Where has this universe gone? By whom has it been removed? It was seen by me before, but it is not. What a wonder! There's only the ocean of bliss. What is to be discarded, what is to be accepted? What is different? What is distinct in this great ocean filled with the nectar of infinite bliss? I do not see anything. I hear nothing. I do not know anything. I simply abide in the form of my own Atman and continue in the enjoyment of Bliss.

"My obeisance to you, O Guru, again and again. O you great one, free from all attachment, the best among the knowers of Brahman, who is the embodiment of the eternal essence of bliss, the infinite, the everlasting supreme reservoir of mercy. By the bestowal of whose gracious glance, like the compact rays of the cool moon, all my afflictions of samsara have been removed, and I have acquired in a moment the undecaying state of the Self, which is of the nature of Infinite Bliss. I am blessed. I attained my purpose. I have been liberated from the clutches of the ocean of birth and death. I am of the nature of permanent bliss. I'm full, by your grace.

"I am Brahman, which is without anything to equal it, the beginningless truth beyond all imaginations and of the nature of uniform eternal bliss, the Supreme Truth. By the play of the winds of maya, the various waves of the universe arise and are merged in me, the infinite ocean of bliss. Like the sky, I am beyond all imagined divisions. Like the sun, I'm different from the illumined. Like the immovable mountain, I'm permanent and unmoving. Like the ocean, I'm without a shore. In my great dream in the forest of birth, old age and death, rocked by Maya, I had got exhausted by various afflictions which afflict me every moment. I have been tormented by the tiger of ego. By your infinite grace, my Guru, you have awakened me from sleep and saved me."

May our Guru also awaken us from the dark night of Maya into the Eternal Sunshine of God-realization. That is my prayer.

www.ingramcontent.com/pod-product-compliance
Lightning Source LLC
LaVergne TN
LVHW051737080426
835511LV00018B/3120